"Read this book carefully, or it'll explode in your hands. Mark Steele has written a book that reads in much the same way that God works in our lives. We don't learn in linear fashion; we learn in hindsight, as memories percolate and themes emerge across disparate events. Don't be fooled by the crazy formatting and hilarious stories—something very serious is going on here."
—**Patton Dodd,** author of *My Faith So Far: A Story of Conversion and Confusion*

"Highly creative yet profound."
—**Margaret Feinberg,** author of *Twentysomething: Surviving and Thriving in the Real World*

"I laughed out loud. I cried. My soul was fed. I love the ending."
—**Victoria Jackson,** actress, former cast member on *Saturday Night Live*

"Somewhere, there's a list of books that artfully combine good writing, laugh-out-loud humor, and cheese-free spiritual content. This list is embarrassingly short. But thanks to Mark Steele and *Flashbang*, it just got a little longer."
—**Jason Boyett,** author of *Pocket Guide to the Apocalypse*

"I have known Mark Steele as a talented multimedia entrepreneur. *Flashbang* will bring his wit and wisdom to a whole new audience."
—**Mark Joseph,** author of *Faith, God & Rock 'n' Roll*

*flash*BANG

mark steele

*flash*BANG

how i got over myself

[RELEVANTBOOKS]

Published by Relevant Books
A division of Relevant Media Group, Inc.

www.relevantbooks.com
www.relevantmediagroup.com

Design by Relevant Solutions
Cover design by Mark Arnold
Interior design by Jeremy Kennedy

Library of Congress Control Number: 2005902183
International Standard Book Number: 0-9760357-2-3

For information or bulk orders:
RELEVANT MEDIA GROUP, INC.
100 SOUTH LAKE DESTINY DR., STE. 200
ORLANDO, FL 32810
407.660.1411

05 06 07 08 9 8 7 6 5 4 3 2 1

Printed in the United States of America

To Kaysie

May we leave beautiful
teethmarks together.

contents

acknowledgments

This account could not have been lived or subsequently recorded for posterity on paper without the grace of my Lord and Savior Jesus Christ and the help of the names that follow:

My beautiful wife and "forever love" Kaysie—when we lived this, it didn't always seem so fruitful—and now here we are. Thank you for being my undying support and for always steering me toward the truth.

Morgan, Jackson, and Charlie. You are my greatest joy—my laughter—my miracle. I want you to know who I am.

My parents, my brothers, and their families. You have molded me and taught me how to laugh. I love you. Thank you for rescuing me and letting me share the story.

The Dodds. Every son-in-law should be so lucky.

The Steelehouse gang: Kevin & Tonya, Jeff, Sam, Juliana, Eric & Nathalie, Paul & Becca, and Mandy. The road begins.

Pastor Roger Nix & Jason Jackson. My friends and accountability.

Patton and Jeff. The best writers I know.

And to Granddaddy—who first told me I was a writer before I had written a single word.

*flash*BANG   (not quite 1i)

prelude to a concussion
—OR—
"PRETENDING"

After sharing a bedroom for more than a decade, you could imagine my surprise when I received the phone call informing me that my brother did not remember me.

Not that I was a stranger to having my name forgotten. As the third of four brothers, my father often called me either Brad, David, Matthew, or Nancy (though I had no sibling named Nancy) before remembering that he himself had named me to begin with and that my name was actually Mark. Of course, once he recalled the name, he would often forget why he was calling me in the first place and instead request that I put away his socks.

My brother's, however, was a very different sort of amnesia. Dav (who has intentionally left the "e" off the end of his name for fifteen years) had been playing flag football at college in Oklahoma and was pummeled in the side of the head, a skull ramming his temple. He was down for about three seconds, then quickly leaped like a gazelle to his feet and huddled for the next play. His teammates were perplexed, but chose to assume the best. When the next ball was hiked, Dav ran down the field in the opposite direction, jogging pleasantly, as if needing to jaunt to the grocery. His teammates then hurried him to the emergency room. From that point, his condition continued to deteriorate until the phone rang, informing us in Georgia that he was in a hospital halfway across the country—and that he had lost his memory. Dav had a severe concussion.

Before my brother's incident, my only association with amnesia had been its effective use as a plot device on television. Sitcoms had been my schooling in many areas. For example, it was in this specific pop-culture medium that I discovered the following life lessons:

*flash*BANG

xiii

- Neighbors eavesdrop on all conversations.
- Life is performed live in front of a studio audience.
- Parents out-of-town equals crazy party.
- All problems resolve in exactly twenty-two minutes.
- A conk to the head causes amnesia.
- A second conk to the head cures amnesia.

All of this memory-loss hyperbole ended up being a crock. I know this because in the second grade, I conked the two class bullies' heads together in order to see if they would both forget who they were and suddenly become kind, upstanding young men. At least, I think they were bullies. I don't remember ever actually being tormented by them as much as I remember them smelling funny and bringing sandwiches to school that did not contain wheat. Neither actually lost their memory nor miraculously changed, but there was a lot of bleeding and wheat-free vomit, and I was punished by being forced to eat lunch with the fifth-graders in the cafeteria. At Clubview Elementary School, this was the equivalent of the third circle of hell. My tormentors (or victims, depending upon whose psych evaluation you lean toward) never bothered me again, and I was grounded for one week without my best friend: the television. Instead I sat adjacent to the screen (where I could not see the picture), staring at my own family as they laughed along with Laverne DeFazio. I never again attempted to willfully inflict a concussion.

Dav's concussion, however, did not benefit from my awareness of comedy minutiae. For instance, the doctor chose to go against my recommendation to drop a brick on Dav's skull to jog his memory back, having never seen it work on television himself.

As frightened as I had been by Dav's malady, I was surprisingly disappointed when his memory came back before we had a chance to fly out to Oklahoma to be with him. There had been an initial shock of his condition, but that was followed by a series of fantasies played out in my mind determining how I might maximize this memory loss for my own temporal gain. The next morning, Dav remembered everything. Evidently, all he needed was a little nap. Not quite a remedial breakthrough, but nonetheless effective. The experience had prompted my imagination: What memories could I not bear to live without? Which ones would I love to have removed forever? The scenario was scary and eye-opening—and, for a time, my only definition of the word "concussion."

I did not realize at the time that in my own spiritual life there were two concussions. One involving my memory. The other affecting my ability to shatter and shake.

But, before I could uncover these personal issues, I first had to discover that a concussion had a second definition. A concussion could also be a noisy bout of pyrotechnics.

You see, my childhood saturation of pop culture came in handy as I eventually pursued a career in the fine arts and media. This, as should be obvious, includes stage shows that involve very large explosions.

I am not the individual who actually triggers the stage explosions. That would be the pyrotechnician. They do not actually allow me near gun powder. But I do write the words "insert explosion here" many times into each live theater script. In fact, just to keep it interesting, I tend to exaggerate the nature of the explosion in my descriptions each time a new instance is cited:

First occurrence: LARGE EXPLOSION HERE

Second occurrence: MAMMOTH TREMOR
                            TAKES PLACE

Third occurrence: FRONT ROW MEMBERS'
                            EARS AND NOSES BLEED
                            FROM SONIC EUPHORIA

Fourth occurrence: ENTIRE AUDIENCE
                            SLIGHTLY CONVINCED
                            JESUS HAS RETURNED

And on and on ad infinitum. I don't know where this desire to startle people comes from, but it probably has something to do with the fact that I am what history would call an American Christian. Personally, I prefer to be called a "follower of Christ" as my desire is to pursue Jesus with my heart, actions, and habits. "Follower of Christ" and "American Christian" are supposed to be synonymous terms. Unfortunately, due to the behavior of too many men to count, they are not.

I have passions and goals that I constantly pursue in the firm belief that they are God's plan for my life: to live a life with actions and words that points others to Jesus; to do so with relevance, creativity, and artistic integrity in my chosen field/calling. Mix a preacher with a comedian, and you get an addiction to shock value. That pretty much sums me up—give or take a dozen flaws and peculiarities that we will address later. But that does not yet explain my infatuation with the two concussions.

A pyrotechnic concussion is not an actual explosion. It is simply a deafening noise that sounds like an explosion. There is no actual visual when the device is triggered—no flame, no firework. And there is no damage. Just gunpowder making a boom with no bullet. This feature always astounded me. What good is a pyro sound effect with no pyro visual? That's like thunder with no lightning. A good joke with no punch line.

Bluster with no proof.

So, one afternoon, in my ever-present pursuit of unnecessary factoids, I stumbled upon a piece of information that clarified why there would be a need for such a device.

There is a weapon used by our nation's police force and military that is, in fact, not a weapon. It is a grenade, if you will. One that sounds off a resounding concussion—but the device in question also has a bonus, more perplexing feature: it emanates a stunning bright light that is not actual fire. In other words, our military utilizes a gadget that looks and sounds like devastation without actually causing any. An explosion but not an explosion. A distraction with no destruction. A big noise and a lot of flash that leaves no lasting mark.

It is called the flashbang.

The flashbang grenade is utilized in a situation where the illusion of an explosion is needed without the demolition. Where the show is more important than the reality. Where the first impression is made at the expense of the one that lasts. It looks, sounds, and feels like a grenade, but in essence does nothing that a grenade is supposed to accomplish in the long run. A few moments later, you would never even know the flashbang had been there.

So there is now an understanding of the two definitions of "concussion":

1. A smack to the head that causes one to forget what should never be forgotten.
2. The sound of an explosion without the reality.

And I realize that my spiritual walk has suffered one concussion in order to cause the other.

You see, I have a passion. Whether or not you believe in Jesus, you more than likely share this same passion. It is the passion to move. To shake things up. To incite change. I see those around me who are hurting, and I want to be a part of their solution. Why? Because my heart breaks for them—or, at least, it did once.

I long to leave a residue. An indentation on this world. A scorched mark of what I believe and live on everyone and everything with which I come into contact. But, often, the light show and the bombast of my intentions move the earth but for a moment with nothing left to linger. Many times my attempts at leaving a crater of God result only in leaving a fading echo of my own voice.

My explosions have often been nothing more than flashbangs.

How could this be if my intentions have been so honorable? Why are my concussions nothing more than noise? The answer is both simple and harrowing: because there has been another concussion at work in my mind—and I did not notice it was there.

I have either willingly or unwillingly slowly grown to forget the things that should never be forgotten. I daily allow the world to smack me in the head, knocking little fragments of proof to the ground, never to be noticed or regathered. And the further I get from remembrance, the less my actions have any true effect.

I long to translate real truth, to communicate the big ending, to pass on God's plan. I long to prompt others to action, to affect, to SHOCK! But, in many ways in as many days, the mark I leave withers away. I splash with smoke and mirrors without leaving a permanent indentation of the truth.

And I glance around at the mess those who believe have made, and I cannot help but wonder if I am not alone. So many explosions abound. So few craters are left behind. Instead, those who believe as I believe tend to bear the horrid marks of forgetfulness:

- Life-altering decisions are realized but not lived.
- Epiphanies become regular rituals only to be eventually abandoned.
- Marriages become stale.
- Prayers become repeated incantations stated from memory without thought.
- The world alters us more than we alter it.
- Old sins habitually rear their ugly head.

Jesus Christ has proven to radically change that which seemed unchangeable for two millennia and beyond. In fact, nothing else has proven more effective than God's power to produce legitimate change. This faith is one with verified substance. So, why do we struggle in our own lives to see evidence remain? If the problem is not in the electricity itself, then the weakness must be in the conduit through which the power travels. Any way you slice it: that leaves you and me.

Like it or not, we have a severe concussion.

The stark reality is that Jesus holds the power to change this world, but this world is seeing less and less of Him through the people who bear His name. We have developed the worst kind of memory loss. We do not remember what needs to be remembered, and we try to ignore what should never be forgotten. As a result, when we finally do make a noise, it leaves nothing real in its wake. It is obvious to all who hear that the explosion was a fraud.

If, indeed, the world and this nation have become places that we condemn and criticize more than affect, something is drastically wrong with the example we are living.

This is what I discovered when I took a long look in the mirror. This is why my attempts at true change were falling flat. So, I dug deeper into a few key questions:

- How do I remember what I should never forget?
- How do I stop standing in the way of Jesus?
- How do I make my explosion matter?

In Ezekiel 36:21, God says: "Then I was concerned for my holy name, which had been dishonored by my people throughout the world" (NLT).

I must hold immense influence on this planet that the turns and tides of God's impression upon mankind are held in the balance by my words, deeds, and actions. And here, I struggle with thinking I am of no value. God makes it clear in this concern that He is not referring to evil or unbelievers smearing Him. He is talking about us. That those who say, "I follow Jesus; follow me to Him," while not being responsible to actually live the truth consistently are in essence leading mankind somewhere else that God did not intend. This concerns Him. And it should very much concern us. We must realize that our everyday decisions matter. We must make an effort to remember. We must stop being flashbangs:

- Choosing style over substance
- Communicating truth by false means
- Impersonalizing our faith
- Living by rules we do not take the time to understand

- Looking for the perfect thing to say instead of the right way to live

The day I discovered these realities were part of my methodology was startling. Because the moment one accepts that this is possible truth, one realizes that all the while he thought he was effective, he was actually just pretending.

To this end, the following two-hundred-or-so pages chronicle the nonlinear dissection of my life up to now to discover what has gone right and what has gone wrong. Where did I take the left turns off the straight-and-narrow? And what can be done to set the path straight again?

As I have dismantled my personal history, I have come to the realization that I have stood in the way of Jesus quite often. In revisiting, I have been reminded. Reminded of six terms that tell the whole story (if the reader will be patient):

1   flashBANG
2   teethMARKS
3   dumbSHOW
4   spitTAKE
5   bloodLETTING
6   slapHAPPY

These six will eventually tell the story of how I remembered what I should never have forgotten.

The story of how I left the flashbang in me behind.

And the story of how I got over myself.

Keep in mind that I am a storyteller, not a philosopher, and that comedy tends to be my language of choice. The escapades are true—or mostly true—and living them has allowed God to open my eyes to the message that lies underneath. The stories are both reflection and hope. The thought that all that pomp and circumstance will somehow lead to very real change.

Somewhere in my life, there has to be an explosion that could truly leave a crater.

*flash*BANG

*But what if I don't want the thread that ties the book together
to be an interview with myself?*

Do you think that's really your decision to make?

Of course I do. It's my inner monologue. I shouldn't have to share it.

You said you would do what it takes.

*Yeah. What it takes to write the book in ninety days. Not what it takes to reveal my
every thought to the seventeen people who read this thing.*

Excuse me for being the left brain. I thought the whole idea here was to
be vulnerable in the hopes that a few of the readers would walk away with
answers. Do you really think that will happen if you only speak from a
detached thought process? There has to be at least a speck of your personal
experience. At this point, you aren't accomplished enough as a writer for
the reader's epiphany to be anything other than coincidental.

That was so encouraging, I almost swallowed my uvula.

Just trying to lay the brutal facts out there.

You should write children's books.

So, my thought is to begin with a few of your failures.

failures.

Very nice effect. Starting the sentence off with a lowercase "f."

I thought it was rather effective myself. Thanks for taking notice.

Yes. Failures. Where your realization of truth came too late or not at all.

If it didn't come at all, how could I write about it?

You're a comedian. Certainly you know how to exaggerate.

the stones
—OR—
"WHAT WE CAN DO WITHOUT"

The first time she dialed emergency that year was not as earth-shattering as the second, but nevertheless uncomfortable. That first time, my wife Kaysie was dialing 9-1-1 for the pain inside of me. Me. The Dad.

I always prefer that any danger in the vicinity will first apply to me. At least I do in theory, because I find it easier to suffer physical pain than emotional anguish, which is what happens to me if the physical pain is thrust upon anyone else important in my life. It has only now dawned on me that this makes me selfish, instead of fatherly. But isn't that almost the case with any father: that he takes the weight, the brunt, the pain, the cold slice of pizza for the sake of being (or at least appearing) stronger? I believe a father would bring on the pain at any and all times—welcome it, in fact—for the sake of that ever-elusive impression of strength.

Unless, of course, the pain in question feels like a monkey is attempting to escape from the father's abdomen.

The specific pain that required a call to 9-1-1 started out subtle, like food poisoning (i.e. that which was consumed for a meal is now alive and retaliating from inside—and it is obligated to smell like some sort of cleaning solution whose ingredients include ammonia and something citrus), but digressed quickly. It moved to a very specific pinpoint somewhere in the vicinity of the six-pack of abs I would have if I wasn't so infatuated with cake, and began to dig. Dig. DIG. How do I describe the dig? It's a digging. It's—no, that doesn't work ... It's like a little tickle. You know that little tickle.

Like when a squirrel eats your eye.

There was definitely something wrong. Something incompatible with all that was taking place inside my person. In short, I felt like my insides were chewing themselves outward.

FIRST PAUSE
for important autobiographical information

I have attempted to keep portions of myself from you for at least a page, and I'm certain that I will be alternately successful and unimpressive in my attempts to hide more, somewhat valuable facts. However, I cannot proceed with this (albeit clever) anecdote concerning a rather lengthy physical malady (still a mystery) until I make a confession. By the grace of God, I am many things: some decent, some questionable, some whimsical. But one thing that I am which I am uncertain how to categorize is the thing that many people believe I am only. I alluded to this before, but here it is, laid out plain for the world to see.

I am a comic.

Did you enjoy how I said "a comic" instead of "a stand-up comedian" as if that lends the occupation an air of renaissance? Yes. A comic. I like that. It's not telling jokes. It's not what your uncle does. It's art. Unless your uncle is named Art, in which case, it isn't like that at all.

I am a comic. Not an "angry young man" comic, utterly disappointed by everything and everyone. I am not that. I mean, I am disappointed. From time to time. Often. As a matter of fact, hundreds of times. Let's take this opportunity to name eight of them.

1. *When the primary Christmas present was a parakeet.*
2. *The second time she dialed emergency.*

3. *Two out of three* Matrix *films.*
4. *When the needle was the size of a McDonald's straw.*
5. *The way I respond to other people's faults as opposed to the way I hope they respond to mine.*
6. *Two-hundred-and-twenty-seven pounds!*
7. *When I went back into the woods.*
8. *Bad eggs in Iowa.*

These are disappointments. And sometimes they are, in fact, comedy. But, I am not an "angry young man" comic.

Nor am I a "Christian comedian," a label which I resist because Christian comedians as a rule are not funny—and unfortunately, funny is a necessary sum of the parts of a comedian. So, I am not a Christian comedian. I am a follower of Christ. And, thank God, sometimes I am funny for profit, gain, and unhealthy doses of adoration by others. I did, however, participate in a Christian comedy tour during the year 1994. And we did, indeed, take a brief but life-altering stop in Iowa. This brings us back to the first time I had food poisoning, which, again, is not the mystery illness I am building toward in the "digging" story that began the chapter, but IS important to where we are going. I cannot convince you of this. You will simply have to trust me.

So quickly—before I resume the mystery—I will refer to the time years prior that I came face to face with bad eggs in Iowa.

I have nothing against Iowa. One of my closest friends in the world is from Iowa. That's not necessarily his fault. But I am disappointed in Iowa's preparation of omelettes. For instance, a Denver omelette should, when prepared with knowledge, include *diced* ham, *sharp* cheddar cheese, and eggs *that will not kill you.*

Well, I simply hurled for days.

And understand that this was the deep-cleansing, brace-your-knees-on-the-toilet-spine sort of throwing up. The sort that is exaggerated over generations into a tale of one brave soul losing his lunch so violently, the large intestine urps outward, unscrolling into the crack of a whip, single-handedly flaying a wildebeest. Nevertheless, the bad eggs were a process that began with a pinpointed ache in the abs. This same ache was the one returning to frighten me the night Kaysie called emergency.

The location of the pain was reason enough to consider this new, dingo-gnawing-on-my-liver sensation the product of a bad meal. I obsessed on the pain, lying there in the fetal position next to my sleeping and pregnant wife at three in the morning. It simply had to be an extreme case of food poisoning (*it wasn't—and I tell you this only to regain the air of mystery that I sense is being lost on you*). I made my way to the bathroom and waited for my Extra Value-Sized meal to take leave.

Waiting. Nothing. Waiting. Nothing.

I finally realized that whatever was holding on was holding on hard, and that my lunch was going to lollygag[1] around until I asserted myself into the process. So I tensed every muscle I could avail and gave my intended one-way meal a round-trip ticket. In other words, I made my best attempt to throw up.

But, how should I say—something caught.

I suddenly became blinded by my own pain, an intense piercing deep into my gut. It was the first time during a sickness that I had the thought "something is very wrong." I felt myself turn blue then green then white, but before I succumbed to the growing onslaught of fainthood, I crawled (no joke, literally tugging at the carpet strands for leverage) back to my bed and awakened my pregnant wife.

Note of caution: never wake up pregnant people (you will notice I used the term "people" as to not blame one specific gender). My wife is a gentle woman—kind, very much like Jesus. But put a baby in her, and you might as well invest in gauze and bactine. Not that she wounds me out of anger when she is pregnant—she does not. She wounds me out of clumsiness. This is why one should never put a pair of scissors in a woman's hand during a season in which she has no peripheral sightline.

1 lollygag (v.): the act of hanging around for no obvious reason: a word—not invented—but proliferated by my father, who has gone by the name of "Butch" for sixty-five years against his will.

But, of course, I woke her up anyway because I could not breathe (which is slightly above mortal flesh wounds on the list of damage). She woke up in a spasm of flailing and was instantly taken aback by the color in my face, as it matched the hue of most dead bodies. This is when she dialed emergency.

The birthday party had hit the three-quarter lull, when most desert the festivities and head out to a movie. This was when Hal pulled out the bucket of freezing cold water from the melted ice and said: Who Wants To Play Pregnancy Test?!

Desiring to seem masculine, I didn't hesitate for the rules to make my intention known. Before it dawned on me that Pregnancy Test might not be a testosterone-fueled competition, I was in.

The emergency number is 9-1-1—or if you memorize phone numbers by their corresponding letters on the dial, it is **YAA!** The barely lifelike person on the other end of the phone picked up and asked my wife if there was an emergency she would like to report. Kaysie informed her that I could not breathe. The emergency woman responded that this was not a good thing. My wife concurred with this state of not-goodness. Emergency woman then confirmed that all parties were in agreement in regard to the growing state of emergency. I, in the meantime, was growing more and more aware of the weight of my spleen and seeing visions of friends and relatives at the end of a bright tunnel.

Kaysie asked what should be done in regard to the dilemma of no apparent oxygen traveling to my brain. To this question, the emergency girl responded *to keep an eye on me.*

Keep an eye on me.

At the risk of being redundant, I would like to truly relish the ridiculousness of that comment and linger one line longer.

Keep an eye on me.

KAYSIE: BUT HE CAN'T BREATHE!
9-1-1:   *Yes. And if he still can't breathe in the morning, feel free to bring him in to the hospital.*

Over the course of the next hour, my struggle did taper off into something more manageable, but I continued to feel deeply nauseated—not to mention upended by the radical path the pain had taken. It was so completely sudden. It astounded me that whatever was shuffling my intestinal tract had snuck up so. That it had gone previously undetected—up until the point where I literally felt I would die. Or at least be ripe for bruising.

The good news: the next morning, Kaysie and I began the day at the medical facility. The bad news: it was Saturday, and the only attendants on duty were interns. A couple of thirteen-year-olds wearing lab coats walked in with clipboards and began grilling me as to my condition. I trusted the status of their doctor coats, even though they were technically younger than my breakfast. After assessing the description of my ailment, they left the room together to debate and returned with angry looks. The subsequent travesty went something like the following dialogue:

"The Diagnosis" Act I, Scene 4

KAYSIE: So, doctor, what's the problem?
INTERN #1:   *Why don't you tell us what the problem is?*
MARK: Because I'm not a medical professional.
                I don't know the problem.
INTERN #2:   *Of course you do.*

(An extended awkward silence.)

MARK: No. I really don't.
INTERN #2:   *I think you do.*

(An awkward silence that rivaled the first in length.)

KAYSIE: Doctor, why don't you just tell us what the
             problem is.
INTERN #1:   *Miss, how well do you know your husband?*
KAYSIE: Excuse me?
INTERN #2:   *What Intern #1 is trying to say, Miss, is that your
             husband has an issue.*
MARK: Yeah. It's called a rodent feeding on my vital
             organs!
INTERN #1:   *Again, Miss, how well do you know your
             husband?*
KAYSIE: Just get to the point.
INTERN #1:   *Sir, based on your age and description, there is
             only one way you could be feeling the pain you
             described.*

(More silence.)

MARK: And?

INTERN #1:   *The only way you could be feeling what you described—the ONLY WAY ...*

INTERN #2:   *... is if you were abusing cocaine.*

(Pause of excruciating length.)

MARK: What do you mean by abusing?

KAYSIE: Do not make jokes about this, Mark! My husband does not do cocaine! There has to be something else!

INTERN #1:   *Nope. Nothing. That's the only thing.*

MARK: There has to be something else because I've never done cocaine in my life.

INTERN #2:   *That's what all cocaine addicts say.*

MARK: Wouldn't it also be what all people who have never done cocaine say?

KAYSIE:	MY HUSBAND DOES NOT DO COCAINE! What are other possibilities?
INTERN #1:	*None. It's cocaine.*
MARK:	Aren't you people supposed to be the healers?
INTERN #1:	*No one's listening to you, cokehead.*
KAYSIE:	We want a second opinion.
INTERN #2:	*Oh. Well—I think it's cocaine, too.*

We left—none the better for an afternoon that, despite all arguments, did not include narcotics of any kind, not even a cough drop. We returned home, having no medical direction, no explanation for the malady, and having actually written a check to pay for being insulted. All the while, I could not help but think: what have I done to give someone the impression that I'm sniffing the magic dust?

The object of Pregnancy Test is for all the real men to submerge one of their naked arms under the icy water— a pain that simulates childbirth. Whoever stays under the longest is the winner!

I had always been drawn to this sort of competition— one that does not require talent or athletic prowess. I had not been an accomplished athlete as a child and had, in fact, only excelled at dodgeball due to the fact that I had a large, resilient skull and didn't mind offering to be all-time target.

I was VERY bad at all other sports. So, always looking for an opportunity to appear tough without any actual physical strain, I answered "yes" to this challenge. I plunged my appendage into the arctic and subsequently began to understand what it might feel like if a Kodiak bear was given free reign to suck on my arm.

A few weeks later, the pain in my abdomen returned. The second time, it was piercing and specific, and I was able to pinpoint its whereabouts to our family physician with greater accuracy.

MY doctor—the SMART one—knew IMMEDIATELY that I was not on cocaine. I was neither then nor previously doing the nose candy. So, in order to confirm his suspicions, he gave me an ultrasound, which confirmed two things:

1. It's a boy.
2. My source of pain was gallstones.

One hundred and four gallstones, to be exact. They were ripping me apart from the inside out, and I never even knew they had arrived.

"The Diagnosis" Act 2, Scene I

MARK:	Doctor, I don't know what gallstones are.
DOCTOR:	*They are very painful round objects formulated in your gall bladder.*
MARK:	You do realize the first adjective you used was "painful."
DOCTOR:	*The first adjective I used was "very." The second was "painful."*
MARK:	Technically, "very" is not an adjective.
DOCTOR:	*I'm a doctor, Steele. Not the grammar police.*
MARK:	How did this happen to me?
DOCTOR:	*We normally don't find these in anyone your age. No. I would have to say these stones are hereditary. Your father had them when he was in his early thirties and so, now, do you. Hooray.*
MARK:	What can be done about them?

| DOCTOR: | *Unfortunately, nothing can be done to dissolve them. We will simply have to remove them and the gall bladder that creates them before you begin to feel the pain.* |
| MARK: | But I've already felt the pain. |

(The doctor laughs slightly and then disguises this with a cough.)

DOCTOR:	*Oh, you think you've felt the pain. You haven't felt squat.*
MARK:	Could you describe the pain I may soon feel?
DOCTOR:	*Well, you've seen the McDonald's golden arches, haven't you?*
MARK:	Yes. Yes, I have.
DOCTOR:	*Take them and tie them into a pretzel knot. Then coat them in an acid-based adhesive affixed with a thousand carrot peelers pointing straight out. Follow that up by removing the head off fourteen life-size replicas of the Statue of Liberty and affix those heads with the pointy helmets on each corner of the apparatus. The next step would be to set the entire device aflame. You got that?*
MARK:	Yes.
DOCTOR:	*Now, shove it through your urethra.*
MARK:	So, looking at other options, then?

I basked in what could only be described as ignorant glee as many masculine types were failing the Pregnancy Test—pulling arm upon arm away from the hypothermia. I acknowledged I was reaching crisis pain, while simultaneously approaching birthday prize euphoria.

My last remaining opponent and I eyed one another, secure in the fact that the other would not, in fact, win when, suddenly, what then seemed a miracle (and now seems nonsense) occurred: I no longer had any feeling in my submerged arm. This was terrific! I could remain here, standing at this Igloo Cooler all night, in a puddle of my own waste, if necessary. Nothing could rob me of the joy of my impending win.

Nothing, of course, but Hal, who returned—shocked we were still playing the game and warning of the impending danger of amputation.

Well. There's one at every party.

There was no other option. The decision was made to remove both the gall bladder and the 104 stones gathered at its opening waiting patiently to stampede their way into my devastation. Emergency surgery would take place the moment I was cleaned out.

The cleaning out in question was a complete excavation from my person of anything I might have eaten or even considered eating in the previous twenty-seven years. This was to be accomplished through consuming just a few drops of a miracle cleanser inserted into juice, which would make its way to my stomach where it would evidently play the part of Samson slaying a thousand Philistines with the jawbone of a donkey.

Twenty-four hours later, I was evacuated like a trailer park in tornado alley. The surgery was on.

Surgical procedures are interesting, to say the least, but I was particularly concerned about the invasive nature of this removal. You see, my father, as previously mentioned, went through the same surgery at my exact age. At that time, the surgeons had to practically sever him into thirds to remove the organ in question. There was no upside to this event with the lone exception that the family finally found the television remote control. It took my father weeks to heal. Weeks I (in my state of busyness) did not have to spare.

"The Diagnosis" Act 2, Scene 2

DOCTOR: *Don't worry, Mark. That's the old-fashioned way. They don't crack you open like that anymore.*

MARK: Is "crack you open" the technical term?

DOCTOR: *Well, we don't say it out loud so much.*

MARK: You don't do it that way anymore?

DOCTOR: *NO! Of course not! That would take too long, and doctors are busy. Nowadays, we just make four tiny incisions.*

MARK: Really? Where?

DOCTOR: *Pull your shirt up, and I'll show you.*

MARK: Okay.

DOCTOR: *SWEET MOTHER. On second thought, I'll just draw a diagram over here. There will be a tiny slice here (just above the gall bladder), a teeniney cut here (just below), a fraction of a scratch there (an inexplicable location somewhere below my chest), and then we will take this large curved fishing hook, insert it into the center of your naval, and carve upward about an inch.*

Hmm. The center of my naval.

I don't spend a great deal of time lingering at the center of my naval. But, from the time I have spent there—digging for lint, retrieving a gummy bear I was keeping warm for later—I know that foreign objects do not belong in the center of the naval. I know this because there is a place deep within its recesses that, when touched, causes the individual's eyes to roll into the back of his head. The world and its surroundings are instantly sucked into a vortex of brain tantrums, and one feels an intense tingling in the extremities. This is why, when we meet people for the first time, we shake hands rather than insert our forefinger into their bellyhole.

But this doctor was about to carve me up like a turkey for the holidays, so I began to protest.

"The Diagnosis" Act 2, Scene 2 (Part 2)

MARK: I protest.

DOCTOR: *Oh. You'll be all drugged up. Which, from your record here with our interns, I see you're used to.*

MARK: I DON'T DO COCAINE!

DOCTOR: *I never mentioned cocaine. Interesting.*

(He makes a few marks on my chart.)

You won't feel a thing. Besides, where else would we put the vacuum tube?

MARK: The whatuum what?

DOCTOR: *The vacuum tube. That's how this works, Steele. We stick lasers in here (the above and below incisions) and a camera in here (the inexplicable incision) and a vacuum hose in your naval and chop, chop, chop, suck, suck, suck.*

MARK: Aren't there other things in there?

DOCTOR: *Don't you worry your pretty little head about those. The things that are necessary will stay good and put. This is why before we withdraw anything, we pump you up with a little extra oxygen.*

MARK:	In layman's terms, define "a little extra."
DOCTOR:	*The equivalent of nine footballs.*

MARK:	# HEY!
DOCTOR:	*Whoa!*

MARK:	NINE FOOTBALLS?! I'll look like a dirigible!
DOCTOR:	*See, now I'm a doctor, and I don't even know what a dirigible is, so how could it be bad?*
MARK:	It's a blimp. Like the Hindenburg.
DOCTOR:	*No idea.*
MARK:	So, what happens to that little extra oxygen afterward?
DOCTOR:	*We'll get most of it out.*
MARK:	Most of?
DOCTOR:	*Oh dear—look at the time.*
MARK:	What happens to the oxygen not included in "most of"?
DOCTOR:	*Well—It will have to pass the way God intended it to.*

GET YOUR ARMS OUT OF THE WATER NOW!
Or something of that equivalence was screamed by Hal,
who, we continued to point out, urged us to put our arms
in the subzero water to begin with.

He had neglected to inform us that Pregnancy Test,
when pursued past the ten-minute mark, could lead to
hypothermia and potential amputation.

Which, in my mind, is when it stops being a GAME.

My opponent and I eyed one another, negotiating an exact-same-moment withdrawal. We did so, and where we expected accolades of manliness from the crowd, instead received chastisement for childish behavior. I'm telling you, this party was LAME. Neither my comrade in frozen arms nor I could understand the big deal as we had completed the task with no pain whatsoever, just a limp limb each bouncing uncontrollably by our sides.

Then—the thaw came.

The moment I was most looking forward to, of course, was getting knocked out by the medication. I had a lot on my mind and, therefore, took what peaceful sleep I could get. I expected to doze for a refreshing mid-morning nap, awakening with a stretch and smile in a room filled with daisies, kittens, and a fruit-based frozen drink involving tiny paper umbrellas. They don't really prep you with accurate details for the moment you awaken.

The reality, of course, is that you do not feel the sleep at all. You count to ten, and somewhere in the middle, you feel your eyes grow heavy, close, and then open wide in the deep dark recesses of sheer and utter pain. No nap—just mountains of lost time. To make matters more disconcerting, when you awaken, there are at least eight doctors surrounding you, none of whom you have ever met—as if you were drugged up and whisked away to another hospital where strangers who do not mind if you die are the ones chosen to cut you open. When these mystery surgeons realize you are coming around, they SHUSH one another quickly—which, of course, brings mountains of encouragement.

SURGEON:	*Mr. Steele. I am Doctor Hgnsqgrnklvx, your surgeon. If you can hear me, please repeat my name.*
MARK:	Dfgsjfdbfiuh.
SURGEON:	*Excellent. He is coherent.*

(Four different men scribble on clipboards.)

	How exactly are you feeling?
MARK:	Well—as if my naval has been pierced.
SURGEON:	*Mmhm.*
MARK:	And attached to that piercing is a small chain.
SURGEON:	*Yes.*
MARK:	And hanging from that chain is a small Norwegian man.

The next moment I actually remember was awakening a second time in my hospital room with sustenance awaiting. I have intentionally avoided the word "meal" as the delicacies in question were chicken broth and cherry gelatin. I gazed to my side and saw that I was on a steady IV of medication.

Kaysie was thrilled to see me come around as she was both anxious to get to the pharmacy to pick up my prescription and nauseated by the appearance of my dinner. Once she realized I was coherent, she fled.

Time passed. I consumed the soup and gelatin treat. I noticed my chest had been shaved. I decided that, as the surgery was on my abdomen, Doctor Hgnsqgrnklvx must have too much time on his hands. I admired the rubber sheets on the bed, thinking that an interesting way to keep a sleeping space cool in the summer. In other words, I was infinitely bored.

Then suddenly, full circle. That little tickle.

The dripping medication mixed with the broth and gelatin was not settling so well, and I realized that I was very rapidly going to have a need to throw up.

Throwing up, of course, comes slowly—in several stages. The first of which is denial.

> *I don't have to throw up. I don't know what this current sensation is, but it is certainly not a need to throw up. I've never thrown up before. Why would I possibly need to throw up now?*

Then, comes acceptance.

> *Oh, I'm going to throw up more passionately than any manner of man or beast since time began. I am going to throw up, down, and all stages in between. I am going to throw up professionally.*

Finally, comes regurgitation. I pulled myself away from the entrapments of the hospital bed and shuffled as quickly as I could toward the bathroom doorjamb while Sven swung precariously from the chain affixed to my naval. It was not until I reached the door itself that I froze, making what would seem to anyone else an obvious discovery.

> *Oh.*
> *I can't bend.*

> *It was as if every droplet of blood in my body had rushed into the arm and was confusedly attempting to shove its way out. My arm, throbbing and thawing from the freeze of the Pregnancy Test, felt as if it were going to fall off at any second.*

> *I rolled into the fetal position in the corner of the park gazebo and cradled my arm as if it were a newborn*

kitten, pleading to God for the ability to fly backward
around the earth at the speed of light in order to turn
back time to a day and hour when I was not a complete
and utter moron. All the while thinking to myself...

You see, in my personal history of throwing up, there are certain muscles that I tend to utilize. But this evening in question, these very muscles that would normally need to tense and react had been lasered through, puffed out, and stitched back. In short, there would be no muscle used in the act of throwing up this evening.

Then, as I stood there, immersed in my own misfortune, uncertain of a next step, I heard it. A voice. And I'm quite certain to this day that it was God Himself.

> *Mark.*
> *You're the sick person.*
> *There's no way you'll have to clean any of this up.*

So I stood with my feet shoulders-width apart as I was taught in gym class, and, like Pavarotti, I saaaaaang it out. I threw up from the diaphragm.

And I kid you not. It arched perfectly.

Up. Out. Into the flawless form of a rainbow like Free Willy set to a Michael Jackson tune. Then, it landed in the toilet bowl with nary a splash nor a sploosh. Zero mess. I believe it even flushed itself.

I stared, stunned.

All this time I was some sort of vomit savant.

Before I could return to reality, a noise from the entranceway of my hospital room commanded my attention.

It was the sound of applause.

Kaysie had returned and witnessed the entire encounter. She stood, amazed in ovation, and stopped to say only one thing:

THE EXTRA POINT IS GOOD!

And there the amusing point of the story ends, for it took my body quite
some time to return to normal, having been invaded, yes, by the knife
and hands of a man whose name consisted exclusively of consonants, but
also invaded by bad little pieces of me—pieces that had grown slowly and
undetectedly—poisons eating away at the very essence of who I was while I
never even felt ill.

For the next several days, I lay on the sofa and coddled my abdomen as
if it were a newborn kitten, pleading to God for the ability to fly backward
around the earth at the speed of light in order to turn back time to a day
and hour when I was not blinded by the pain that had been growing inside
of me. All the while thinking to myself ...

----

*... how did I not feel this pain coming when it was
creeping up silently the entire time?*

So, what were they?

What were what?

Your gallstones.

*They were small, hard, pathological concretions, chiefly made of cholesterol
crystals, formed in the bile duct.*

I'm not looking for the definition you found in Gray's Anatomy.

Then, what do you mean?

What were your gallstones really?

They were really gallstones. The story is true.

I know the story is true. But that's not why you told the story. What else were your gallstones?

Besides actual gallstones?

You know what I mean. This book isn't a collection of humorous essays with no purpose. The story is here for a reason. You clearly intend to bring out an analogy so the reader desires to go back and review the chapter again under a new and more meaningful context. Correct?

How do you know these things?

So—what were *your* gallstones?

I imagine that would be difficult to narrow down, but—

Spit it out.

My thought life.

Interesting. Not something more tangible. More—concrete?

Well, I think—for anyone—the concrete manifestations aren't the real infection. They're just indicators.

Of?

I mean, you run into people with their primary issue: for some it's pride or greed or substance abuse or lust, or in this culture God only knows how many other things stand in our way—that mute us—that make our potential example impotent—but those things aren't the real core of the infection. They just flow out of it.

The real infection runs much deeper.

But—your thought life?

My struggles have always been the extrapolations of my mind—worries, stress, doubt, fear, lack of self-worth—this had, at times, turned into other habits that fed that disease, but they began with the reality that I wasn't taking Paul's words to heart in Philippians to let God's peace guard my heart and mind as I live in Christ Jesus. To worry about nothing—instead pray about everything—telling God what I need and thanking Him for all He has done. When I stewed instead on the preoccupations of my mind, the disease crept in unnoticed like a small stone or a slow freeze until I would eventually reach the point of despair, seemingly suddenly, having no idea how I got there and, therefore, having no idea how to get out.

And the despair made matters worse.

Next thing I knew, one small stone became 104, and I'm throwing up, doubled-over with pain, realizing slowly that there is no quick fix—I'm just numb from the freeze, knowing the only comfortable place is to stay infected, that healing means intense pain for a season. But, of course, to stay comfortable is to eventually die or be an amputee, so I choose instead to suffer a dozen cuts and procedures that will lay me in bed for a few weeks until one day I'm able to walk and eat again. The pain is gone, but the scars will always stick around as reminders.

But isn't coming to Jesus *about* transformation?

I do believe there is an instant change that man cannot fake or create. The power of God does transform, but what that really looks like has been radically miscommunicated. There is an insinuation that when your sin gets the best of you, run to God, and He will miraculously make all better, no problem. That on Saturday you're running into destruction and Sunday running into the arms of God and that there is no road or pain in between the two. That simply isn't true, and it shouldn't be true because God isn't concerned with us feeling good. He's concerned with us growing in character—and pushing through the pain of adversity to make the right decision is what makes us men and women of character. *God loves the road in between the two because He cares more for what we become than the big finish. It is a necessary process. God's people in the Old Testament were ridiculously hard-headed. They would turn their backs on God on a regular basis and then come back pleading to Him on their knees. On one such occasion, they came to a prophet and begged him to tell God that they would "make up" for their sins by giving Him thousands of their best cattle—that they would sacrifice their children to Him if it would fix their situation. The prophet answered, "No. The Lord has already told you what is good, and this is what He requires: to do what is right, to love mercy, and to walk humbly with your God." He didn't allow an easy way out. He said, if you feel guilty, don't try a quick fix. Do what I have already told you to do.*

They were flashbangs.

Aren't we all? Aren't we all until the moment we take the action we have been avoiding? We can keep trying to finish God's plan our own way because it is, in our opinion, the most pleasant, but it will never actually lead to anything. We try to make something out of it, but the explosion leaves no impression. If we truly want to leave a mark, He has already told us what to do.

We have to choose His plan.

It doesn't matter how good or bad our plan is. If it isn't God's plan, it's just going to turn into a series of stones that eventually tear us inside out.

So—first, we recognize that we need surgery.

We have to realize that many of those things we've always said we stand against—that some of them are currently inside of us.

But that still doesn't answer the question.

What makes you think I have the answer to the question?

You say there are infections inside of us—things we must do without—
that, instead, we tend to hold onto because we are afraid of the pain of
switching over to God's plan.

Correct. But, I think I missed the question.

How do we know what God's plan is?
How do we cut those gallstones out?

That would be the next chapter.

the effect of cages
—OR—
"HAMSTER—THOU ART LOOSED!"

Yes. Once, the primary Christmas gift was a parakeet. And you have to keep in mind that the receivers of this gift were four boys. Three of the boys already in their teens. Late teens.

You also have to keep in mind that we asked for electronics.

The parakeet was blue. And afraid. Blue and afraid. And his excrement looked like those little kernels in salami, of which I am no longer fond.

He was both uninteresting and too much of a conversationalist. And selfish. Let's not forget selfish. Wanting nothing to do with his four owners' little stunt training.

And his name was Sam. Sam the parakeet. The primary Christmas present. Not a bad present if you enjoy sitting quietly and staring at a cage, which the four strapping boys did not enjoy at all. For Sam, the cage was a protective covering. A way to enjoy the outside world without being vulnerable to it. For the four boys, the cage was an obstacle to get past in order to release a toy that would never need batteries.

You see, upon receiving a Christmas gift that was not on the lists, the first natural response for a gaggle of sons is disappointment. But, the follow-up response is, of course, creative repurposing. Yes. I asked for a remote-controlled airplane and received a parakeet. But how might this parakeet make a good remote-controlled plane? Other sons considered the bird's potential uses as an action figure, a homing pigeon, or a piece of equipment for badminton. Suddenly, the gift seemed fun and unpredictable. That is, as soon as we could get it out of its cage.

So, on Christmas Day—the first moment the bird lived in our house—we decided to pull the bird out of the cage in order to make the most of the situation. Not realizing, of course, that when a bird has never lived a day outside of a cage, the real adventure begins when you attempt to put him back inside.

Parakeets are funny things, too. While they are inside the cage, they seem innocuous, even a little bit boring. They sit quietly on the perch, staring at you with their head slightly cocked to the right. This is not, however, the case when they are loosed from their cage. When they are released—

SWEET MOTHER!

The dive-bombing! The SQUAWKS! The frantic flittering of the little blue wings toward one's face. And that beak! THAT BEAK! THAT INSTRUMENT-OF-DEATH BEAK!

The beak cuts through cans.

A parakeet undergoes utter transformation out of the cage. Why? Because, for one brief moment—IT STOPS BEING A PET! It becomes as much a proprietor of the premises as you because YOU CAN'T CATCH IT! YOU CAN'T PUT IT BACK IN THE GOD-FORSAKEN CAGE!

We tried for three full hours.

We made attempts to safely capture Sam and replace him before the parents noticed. By "safely" I mean only that we did not get into trouble. The "safely" in question did not necessarily apply to the bird itself. To this end, the trapping of Sam was accomplished by a mixture of attempts utilizing the following tools:

1. tissues
2. a coat hanger
3. a wiffle bat
4. screaming
5. candy
6. an empty paper towel roll
7. diversionary tactics
8. a pillowcase

Original attempts to pick Sam up with (1) led to bites on our fingers that angered us into utilizing a mixture of (3) and (4); (4) proved disorienting enough to pursue (6) in hopes of tricking him with (7) into a fake escape tunnel lured by (5) which, after many failed attempts, we ate ourselves. We then attempted to seize him in our naked hand, which led to more biting and much more (4) (1) and (3). Finally, we found a way to utilize a mixture of (3) (2) and (4)—always (4)—to nudge him into (8), dumping (8) back into the cage while cleaning up mountains of budgie poop with all the remaining (1) in the house and celebrating with a lot of (5) and one more round of (4).

And, of course, the moment he landed in the cage again, he became motionless and quiet as a mouse. That parakeet had met its match in four human beings with a myriad of tools.

We didn't really mean it when we said make a wish. It's just what parents say to little girls who belong to them and are about to turn five. But Morgan made a wish and then told a friend that what she had wished for was a hamster.

The idea of a hamster is simple enough. It only has one job—to be cute. So my wife and I caved and, for her fifth birthday, gave Morgan a brand new hamster. A hamster she named—ironically—Sam.

This hamster was, by sheer math, a good gift. By math, I mean that it had three positives and one negative.

Three positives: It was small. It was cuddly. It was quiet.

One negative: It was dying.

For the next three months, I eyed that parakeet with an air of suspicion. What did he do in the dark of night? Did he make plans of escape? Did he ever close that one cocked eye? Did he hold a grudge because of the infamous coat hanger deception (for which it came to be known)? For this very reason, I did my best to pass the cage swiftly, never making direct eye contact. I would only slip his food into the feeder if he were several feet up the cage and could not swoop down and take out a finger like one might consume a Vienna sausage. I avoided him and pretended he did not exist.

That is, until the day he called me over.

bird:	*Ker-gleep.*
MARK:	Excuse me?
bird:	*Ker-PLOUND!*
	(slight cocking of the head to the left)
MARK:	Are you talking specifically to me?
bird:	(nothing)
MARK:	This is amazing. Are you trying to give me some sort of message?
bird:	(nothing)
MARK:	I'll bet you're trying to give me some sort of message.
bird:	(braces himself on the side of the cage and does a flip)
MARK:	YOU JUST DID A FLIP!
bird:	*Ker-gleep.*
MARK:	I JUST TAUGHT YOU HOW TO DO A TRICK! GOOD BIRD! Does the flip mean you want more seed?
bird:	(second flip)
MARK:	Out of the cage? Are you insane? You know I can't let you out of the cage.
bird:	*Ker-PLOUND!* (spastic wing flapping)
MARK:	I know you've changed. But I don't want to get into trouble.

But we both knew I was going to cave. It was just a matter of how many flips he would have to do before I would let him out. The answer, as should be obvious, was five.

Over time, Sam would call to us and flip whenever he wanted out of his small home. We would open the door, and he would jump to our finger, walk all the way up the arm to our shoulder, reach over and KISS US, then fly to a previously assigned spot in the house where he was given free reign to sit and stare with that one eye. Over time, we grew accustomed to his fly-bys and his willingness to unexpectedly land on a visitor's shoulder before he or she yet knew we even owned a Sam. We grew accustomed to finding little salami seed droplets in absolutely everything. We developed a fondness for losing track of him for days at a time, only to have him launch spastically from a lampshade as Mom would reach inside of it. He became one of the family.

Until the night he flew too fast into his own reflection.

We buried him in a Pringles container in the backyard with a little headstone that our six-year-old brother made. I thought the headstone was made out of yellow Play-Doh, but, in retrospect, it might have actually been Velveeta. Either way, it was gone by morning. This moment was devastating and defining and caused every one of the four boys to debate whether or not it had been worth it for the bird to be allowed to live outside of his cage.

Our father—aware that the mood of the house had now transferred from pet frolic into a reluctance to accomplish yardwork—went out and swiftly purchased another parakeet. As if erasing history, we promptly named him Sam as well. We released him into his cage and instantly sat, staring, anticipating his imminent flip.

We waited. But no flip came.

We couldn't be absolutely certain the hamster was dying. That is, we couldn't be absolutely certain until we discovered that he had started to decompose. This was

startling enough without three toddlers standing near,
waiting in line to snuggle with him.

It was our children's first lesson in death. We were,
at that moment, empowered to share with them the
wonders and inexplicable beauty of heaven while they
stared aghast at the rotting corpse of their pet.

My wife led the ceremony as the Samster was buried in
the backyard in one of the three square feet our Black
Lab had not already dug up. Kind words were spoken.
A song, perhaps, was sung. They might have recited the
alphabet. Anything that seemed important.

It was my job, of course, to heal the wounds with my
checkbook and go out and purchase a second, also
unwanted, hamster to replace the docile first. I should
have chosen more carefully. For some reason, the only
defining quality that felt truly important at the moment
was that the second hamster appear similar to the first.

I did not think to make certain that the second hamster
was not possessed by demons.

It seemed months since a bird had flown freely throughout the Steele
home, warming us with its squawk, its mid-air excrement release, its ways
that were beyond our ways. It had not been months. It had, in fact, only
been about eighty-seven minutes—and we had been staring at this second,
less favorite of the parakeets for approximately eighteen of those. This new
parakeet had an inherent problem. It liked that cage. It *loved* it. It preferred
it to us. Yes. That was the real pain, wasn't it? That we were not as good as
the New Sam's little prison. This Sam was ignorant of its own impending

freedom. It was lazy. Hesitant. All the things Steeles were not, unless the television happens to be on. So, in a moment of inspiration, my brother did what any red-blooded American fifteen-year-old would do to a new parakeet moments after the first had died.

He reached in, grabbed him, and threw him into the living room.

I don't know if I've ever *heard* fear quite so distinctly as the moan that came from that bird while he was hurled at the speed of a curveball across the sofa and into the burlap drapes. Sam II caught the curtains with his claws and hung sideways, like the short hand at three o'clock, for dear life.

My six-year-old brother, convinced the bird was simply stuck (as opposed to nearing rigor mortis), plucked him from the drapes and threw him back toward the cage. This time, Sam II caught the wind and flew upward, soaring past his tiny cage and landing on the edge of a lampshade. The lampshade tilted with his weight, frightening him into running around its rim, attempting to correct the tilt back into a perfect horizon. As the correction never quite came, he kept running in that lampshade circle. Around and around and around.

We stared.

The other Sam had been brave. We were perplexed at this new Sam's unwillingness to be thrust into the suburban wilderness. At his sheer lack of fortitude. This Sam was not a parakeet. He was a chicken. Or he was for at least three days.

After three days of being the badminton of our teen existence, Sam II finally got a clue and began to fly—faster, higher, STRONGER than any Sam before. Eventually, we removed the top from Sam's cage because he knew on his own when it was time to return for bed. He followed us about the house the way a puppy might and became one of our closest friends. He played games with us, crawled along our shoulders, arms, and fingers. He squawked happily and joyously, chirping with each sunrise, happy to have a whole home to himself.

He truly lived.

He lived on faster and stronger all the way through high school, on into college—until I was nearing graduation. One evening, as I was studying a subject that I will never utilize in my actual career path, the phone rang. I picked it up, and there, on the other end, was my younger brother, nearing the end of high school himself. He had bad news. Sam II had passed.

MARK:	You're kidding.
MATT:	*Why would I kid about the bird dying?*
MARK:	I don't mean really kidding. I'm just surprised.
MATT:	*Yeah.*
MARK:	You okay?
MATT:	*Sure.*
MARK:	Is Mom okay?
MATT:	*Yeah. She wants to know if you're coming home.*
MARK:	In about a month, yeah.
MATT:	*Not for Thanksgiving. She wants to know if you're coming home now.*
MARK:	Now? For what?
MATT:	*For the funeral.*
MARK:	For the bird's funeral?
MATT:	*Uh huh.*
MARK:	No. I'm not coming home for the bird's funeral.
MATT:	*That's what I figured, but she wanted me to ask anyway.*
MARK:	Sure.
MATT:	*I'm making the headstone.*
MARK:	Block of cheddar?
MATT:	*No. Silly Putty.*
MARK:	Good choice. So uh— was it the mirror again?
MATT:	*Was what the mirror?*
MARK:	Did the bird die by flying into the mirror?
MATT:	*Not the mirror. No.*
MARK:	Well—then, what did he fly into?
MATT:	*A boiling pot of spaghetti.*

SECOND PAUSE
for important autobiographical information

I don't tend to laugh at the things a civilized human being is supposed to laugh at. I do laugh. Often. And loudly. But, when I do, it tends to be at a moment one is not intended to find humorous.

I believe this is due to the fact that I have learned the hard way that what Carol Burnett said is true:

> *"Comedy is nothing more than Tragedy plus time."*

Actually, that might not have been Carol Burnett at all, but I believe I heard it in Undergraduate Theatre History II, which means the individual who said it could have been anyone from Henrik Ibsen (the playwright) to Tom Waite, who sat beside me and is now Michael Vartan's stunt double on Alias. Whether the aforementioned quote was Carol Burnett or not, I do know for a fact that it was Mel Brooks who said an even more poignant line regarding the human condition:

> *"Tragedy is when I cut my finger. Comedy is when you fall into an open sewer and die."*

I did not make these statements up (well, I might have made up the first one), but I do know by experience that they are true. I tend to laugh when others don't. This doesn't mean that I laugh at pain. No. That would be what my wife, Kaysie, laughs at. Not her own pain, mind you. She laughs at my pain. Not all pain. If I were to, for instance, cut my hand, she would be immensely concerned and rush me to the hospital. However, if I were bludgeoned into the ground by a falling tractor, she would have difficulty keeping a straight face. She laughed when I ran headfirst full-speed into our bedroom wall in my sleep. She laughed when I came home from Mexico covered head-to-toe with bandages. She laughed when I could not close my left eye for a month. It's just the way she is built. And I love her for it.

However, most tragedy is not funny at the moment. As I went through the pain of my gall bladder surgery, my brother's concussion, the death of a myriad of pets, and the astounding-but-true incidents yet to be read by you—the moments were indeed painful and pivotal to the man I became. But after these moments were not quite so of-the-moment, they tended to become two completely separate things:

> 1. *Life lessons in analogy form.*
> 2. *Inappropriate humor.*

To this end, I did not intend to laugh when my younger brother informed me that Sam II had flown into a boiling pot of garlic meat sauce and sunk to the bottom like quicksand.

I did not mean to be so cold-hearted. I did not mean to belittle the life of a tiny friend. I did not mean to laugh.

But laugh—indeed I did.

MATT:	*Why are you laughing?*
MARK:	I'm (breath) not laughing (wheeze) at his death. I'm (snort) laughing at the (wipe tear) meat sauce.
MATT:	*It was actually pretty awful.*
MARK:	I would imagine.

MATT:	*Would you want to drown in meat sauce?*
MARK:	No. No, I wouldn't.
MATT:	*Good news is we got to order pizza.*
MARK:	At least he died for a reason.
MATT:	*Yeah.*
MARK:	What did you do with him?
MATT:	*I put him in a Ziploc baggie for Dad.*
MARK:	Careful where you bury him. Raccoons love meat sauce.
MATT:	*Oh. We're not burying him.*
MARK:	You're not?
MATT:	*No.*
MARK:	Then why are you making a headstone?
MATT:	*I guess it's actually more of a memorial.*
MARK:	If you're not burying him, why does Dad want him in a baggie?
MATT:	*To take him back to the pet store.*
MARK:	Take him back to the pet store?
MATT:	*Yeah. Dad wants a refund.*

The girl at the pet store was having a bit of difficulty wrapping her head around the fact that the parakeet was near a boiling pot of spaghetti to begin with. This was not helped by the fact that she was not a veterinary specialist as much as a cheerleader who liked kittens and needed an hourly wage to afford that Garfield tongue ring. Let's call her Melinda.

It turns out, in fact, that you can't get your money back on a parakeet you have owned for seven years—even if it died prematurely by way of Italian food. When asked why, this girl with the Duran Duran T-shirt who worked part time at Jay's Pets at the mall gave three reasons:

1. You simply can't return pets.
2. I don't know how to work the register.
3. Parakeets only have a life span of two years.

We found this line of reasoning impossible as Sam II had lived furtively for seven years and was, in fact, just now blossoming as a stunt pilot. However, Melinda the kitten lover was the "expert," and so Dad came home instead with two smaller birds, each about half the size of the Sams. This selection was made evidently so that the Steeles could sense a new change of pace. This is the reason Dad brought home the finches.

Breaking tradition, Morgan named the second hamster "Squirmy," evidenced by the fact that he wriggled free from the loving touch of any human and, instead, reared back on his hind legs, bared his fangs with a hiss, and pierced the human's skin with his laser vision.

We protested. "But, honey, you have to name him Sam."

"Why?"

"Because all pets named Sam die, and this hamster is the antichrist."

Many other names had been debated for the rodent in question, including "Trouble," "I-have-yogurt-stuck-to-my-booty," and "Third Horseman of the Apocalypse," but the one that stuck was "Squirmy."

The name befitted him in the fact that, where the other hamster had been content to lay in his small cage and internally bleed to death, this hamster was always fidgeting, hankering to get out of its confinement. He was in no way a pacifist. He wiled away his hours—not running in his tiny treadmill—but rather ramming the plastic walls of his cage, testing it for weak spots.

How do I know the hamster yearned for open spaces?
Partly because he continually bit the hand that fed him
(normally while the hand was in the act of feeding him),
but mostly because one cold autumn morning, I awoke
at four in the morning to check on baby Charlie and
found instead an empty cage lifted off its hinges and a
trail of hamster poop that led to certain freedom.

The story of the Steele family's finches has become, in a way, folklore. It is a story I cannot personally validate as I was away at college. This fact will come in handy as now I have free reign to exaggerate. Regardless of the details, the facts of the story that are the most ridiculous are also the ones that are the most true.

Dad named the finches Doris and Henry—after characters in a comedy recording we had heard as children. The names fit the finches well because the characters in the recording had always been bickering—and the primary difference between parakeets and finches is that finches are half as tall and nine times as annoying.

As much as a veterinarian superstar like Melinda would have protested that a parakeet should never be allowed out of its cage, it is even more absurd and atrocious to ever release a finch. A finch simply cannot defend itself in the wild of Butch and Patty's living room. However, rebelling against all animal-wise authority, Doris and Henry were immediately released with the top lifted off their cage, never to be resealed. For days, the tiny birds wouldn't dare to move with the wide-open spaces left unattended above them. But this hesitancy did not last. Eventually, they became as comfortable with my parents' now new and larger home as the Sams had once been with an abode much smaller. Only now, there were two flyers.

They reveled in their aerodynamic showmanship, intertwining their flight patterns and zipping by like Tinkerbell on crack. Their favorite haunt was my father's shoulder, landing there together and often while he was reading the newspaper. They were so familiar and so weightless that he seldom realized they were even there.

Had he noticed the two finches nestling on his shoulder, my father probably would have hesitated to walk out the front door and check the mail. But he did not notice until he opened the mailbox. At that moment— that subtle squeak of the rusty mailbox door hinge—Doris and Henry were startled. Their sudden movement caused my father to turn his head quickly. The turn of his head thrust them off his shoulder. And the finches quickly flew far, far away from home.

Two little domesticated pets out in the actual wild with no cage to which to return and no shoulder to snuggle.

My father stood there, staring off at the two tiny dots disappearing into the horizon. The last of the pets had fluttered away. Dad decided right then and there that one last bird-induced heartache was enough. Doris and Henry would not be replaced.

The last thing I wanted to do was actually inform my wife in the dark of night that Squirmy the Rodent Android from the Third Circle of Hell was free—roaming the nooks and crannies of our house.

It was four in the morning, but certainly I could find that creature if I set my mind to it, and who left this Beanie Baby on the floor?

SWEET MOTHER!

Just as I was about to accidentally step on him, Squirmy sped away, searching for any crevice to hide within. He was too fast for me, but I was able to continually leap ahead of him to block off whatever hole he was escaping toward.

CRASH!

"Mark? What's going on in there?"

"Nothing. I'll tell you in a second."

SMASH!

"It doesn't sound like nothing."

After a large amount of brisk and clumsy movement in the dark, Squirmy escaped. I knew he could not have gone far, because I had sealed every door and hole I could find.

I was perfectly content to have him disappear forever, but I knew it would not fare well with my princess of a daughter who, though often attacked by the creature, adored him still.

I would wait until morning. Sunrise would ferret him out.

Dad was true to his word. He did not return to the pet store, and he did not purchase or pursue another bird or myriad of birds as replacement for the ones lost. He and Mom simply lived their quiet lives with their children off at college in a quiet house free from squeaks, squawks, and bleeps for the first time in more than a decade.

For one year.

Then, one fateful day, my father went outside, once again, to check the mail. He paced his normal routine from the garage door down the driveway. Nothing out of the ordinary. He reached for the mailbox. That same squeaking sound.

Suddenly, out of nowhere, he heard the spastic fluttering of wings near his ear. He glanced over.

On his shoulder sat one small finch. Chirping as if in recognition.

Dad was perplexed and walked back into the house, maintaining the bird on his shoulder. When he opened the front door, the bird hopped off his shoulder, flew through the house room by room, and landed right on the top perch of the opened cage that my parents had never discarded.

It was Henry. The same bird. One full year later.

He went on to live a lengthy and full life, longer than the life of either Sam, even though the textbook lifespan of a finch is even shorter than that of a parakeet.

Why and how could any of our birds have lived that long? To the Melindas of the world, that will remain a mystery. But to me, it is the natural repercussion of what happens when a creature embraces its cage but lives with the roof wide open.

Henry had all the liberty of the skies at his disposal. But, after all was said and done, he decided to return to his coverless cage—because though free reign there was limited, he knew it was truly his home.

Morning came, and, for the life of me, I could not find a clue or a trace of Squirmy's whereabouts. I resigned myself to the fact that he would eventually get very hungry and make himself visible. When he did, I would certainly get a phone call at work from a very rattled Kaysie.

Approximately two and a half hours later, I could tell by the actual sound of the ringing phone that it was a wife in hysterics.

Kaysie had been reaching into a cabinet for a bowl when the rodent appeared, standing on its hind legs and evidently spewing profanities.

He had found a secret place tucked behind the dishwasher. A small hole underneath the cabinets had allowed him to travel there. He had clearly hoped it to be a route of escape. Instead, he discovered a dead end.

Upon my arrival home, the hamster was starving and desperately thirsty, but resisting my hand with everything inside of him. He was a stubborn little cuss, and he was unknowingly burrowing himself into a corner where starvation was the only option. Yet, every time a hand reached out to feed him, he would indeed bite it. His behavior outside of the cage did not differ that much, after all, from his life inside of it.

For hours, the hamster fought against returning to his food, his water, his stuffing bed. He did not want the confines of the cage—not realizing, of course, that he had caged himself now even outside his lair. A cage he had created with his own belligerence. A wall between himself and that which was reaching out to save him. He should have been able to recognize my hand. It smelled of him. It had cuts shaped like his own teeth. And it kept reaching. The same hand. Over and over.

But he resisted.

I wanted to use the vacuum hose. I really did. But my wife said it was a no go.

Man. That would have been great for this story.

Instead, I reached for one of my children's toy butterfly nets. I filled it with his food. I set it within smelling distance. And I waited.

1ii: the effect of cages

And waited.

And waited.

And waited.

get over yourself
—OR—
FLASHBANG SURGERY

I see you've placed the word "flashbang" back into the alternate title of the chapter.

It's called a wraparound. They do it in the movies.

I was beginning to worry. You haven't really mentioned it much.

Certainly I have.

You have?

Haven't you been paying attention? The flashbang is there in all of the stories so far. It's the gallstones. It's the concussion.

Oh. I get it. It's the cage.

Well—no.

What?

The flashbang is not the cage. The cage is good.

The cage is good?

You haven't been paying attention.

How can the cage be good? Don't you read self-help books? "Get out of your cage!" "Free yourself from the confines that hold you back!" "No limits." "Go for broke and reach for the skies!" You're a writer. You should be absorbing these clichés.

I'm certain those catch phrases look great on a poster of a waterfall. But in this story, the cage is good.

And, how can you be so certain?

Because I am the hamster.

Oh.

Yeah. Trust me. I wasn't crazy about the idea of a cage either. There's something about being American or maybe being male or maybe being human that makes me think I deserve unlimited freedom. But unlimited freedom is a big problem.

Call me paranoid, but you've got to be losing some readers right about now.

It's actually quite logical.

Do tell.

Let's lose the term "cage" for a minute and instead call it parameters. I know that I have a distinct purpose in life. I believe God created me for a reason.

And that makes you a flashbang?

NO! The impatience makes me a flashbang!

The what?

The impatience! Trying to achieve my ultimate purpose without the accurate process. Wanting out of the cage or the parameters on day one. That is what makes me a flashbang.

The truth is: each and every one of us is born a wild beast. We live in a nation and a time that celebrates freedom. That's a great thing, but we've celebrated ourselves out of any sort of parameters that keep us from being true. We've given ourselves so many rights and freedoms, we've just about killed ourselves.

This is not going to be a popular philosophy.

Let's follow the path:
God creates man. God gives man freedoms. Freedom to choose. Freedom to grow. Freedom to take God's plan and run with it. But those freedoms aren't enough for man. Man wants more than God wants him to have. Man wants to do whatever he wants to do whenever he feels like doing it. So man chooses freedoms that were not intended for him. And man does whatever he wants to do. But all of those things man does outside God's plan have repercussions. Consequences. Man doesn't like how that feels, so what does man do? Man attempts to create more freedoms that allow him to ignore the consequences created by his old freedoms. Freedoms that allow man to feel better about his excess freedoms. But those new requests for freedom are not accepted by God. So, instead, man decides part of what freedom means is that he has the freedom to redefine God and create a revisionist history of what God said. Time passes. Man embraces his own selected freedoms. Those freedoms evolve from being the abnormal choice into becoming society's widely accepted choice. Those freedoms eventually seep into the church itself and subsequently into the daily lives of followers of Christ—because

the world says how can you believe in a God who loves if
you aren't willing to accept all of our freedoms-of-the-month?

We have become flashbangs because we have accepted these freedoms?

We have become flashbangs because we don't even realize
we are living freedoms that God did not give us.

Ouch.

The lie of "unlimited freedom" is a publicity stunt of the enemy.
God gives "real freedom"—but it is not unlimited.
God knows we are born wild. He creates us that way on purpose.
He isn't looking for us to be domesticated.
He wants us to be free—out in the wild rather than protected from it,
but He wants us to be prepared for that first moment of freedom.
Disciplined and trained for our eventual release.

But eventual could take awhile.

Exactly why so many of us bypass God's process.
I was able to see God's plan for my life, so that made me want
to go after it in my own methods rather than be disciplined in His
methods. It's like the hamster who never went to the water.
He just looked for ways out.
So he gets out to where there's no more water only to
discover he didn't drink enough to get a foot outside the cage.
I embraced the wilderness prematurely
and resisted the cage—the challenge of character development—
that God was trying to train me to climb out of.
It is the very thing that almost killed the hamster.

But the birds lived.

Oh yes! The birds. The parakeets, the finches. They all lived far, far
beyond their normal life spans because they spread their
wings into the wild, all the while returning to the cage to rest and refuel.

So the birds lived longer because they did not resist the cage.

They lived in both worlds.
They spread their wings in one
while finding their source in the other.
Had I only been so smart.
Instead, I spent my time devising ways of escape—
not realizing that everyone has a cage.
Some never leave it. Some never go back to it.
But both of those kinds of people are flashbangs.
The only way to reach those in the outside world is to go there.
And the only way to make that reach accurate and strong
is to return home on a regular basis.

So real freedom has nothing to do with getting away from the cage.

We think our society is so elite because we choose our own freedoms,
but really, we are just in constant denial
of what it means to be a true human being.
We fight against the cage for the sake of freedom,
but we are nothing close to free. We trick ourselves
into believing we are fulfilled, and on the few
days we face reality and discover that we are not,
we burrow into more self-proclaimed freedoms
to make us forget that we are frauds.
We resist. We have no substance.

God made us. God gave us His freedoms, His rules, His plan.
And from the moment we realized that,
we have fought Him on it tooth and nail.

Following Jesus is irony. Always has been.
Be last to be first.
Give to receive.
Be weak to be strong.

Get in the cage to get out of it.
Get fed to get free.

Get under His freedom to get over yourself.
As a follower of Jesus, I will never truly affect the world
with His love until I get over my own desires and needs,
my desperation and petty bickering—anything I cling to in order
to feel better—to feel freer.

I must swallow my pride.
Forget what I believe I deserve.
And get over myself.
Resist the world's freedoms.
Embrace God's parameters.
Allow myself to be accountable and restricted.
Choose to go without every little thing I want.
Strengthen my character.
Determine where I am incorrect.
Humble myself.
Stop manipulating God's way to look like my preferences
and choose His plan—His way—
for every detail.

If I can just deal with life and allow God to use those dealings to
transform me into the right person—the explosive person,
the person with gun powder in my veins—
then the noise I make will be worth hearing.
The fire that is seen in my life will scorch the room.
The substance of my life will pierce the hearts of those around me.

And where I stand, I will always leave a mark.

Because you choose to get over yourself.

It's time to cut myself open
and remove the remains of the flashbang
once and for all.

*teeth*MARKS

So we discover the thing inside that has made us flashbangs.

And we work within God's plan to pluck it out.

But won't that leave a hole?

Of course. You have to fill it with something.

Teethmarks?

That's not the filling. It's just the next step.

Where will these teethmarks actually be left?

You expect me to spoil the ending?

If you do, I won't have to read the whole thing.

Exactly why the answers won't come until after another lengthy anecdote.

Oh goody. Please use more flowery language. I can't get enough of that.

things break
—BUT—
NOT EVERYTHING

The faction of people who have fallen out of a car and landed on their lips is not a very large club, but I am proud to have become a member at the tender age of four.

To be completely accurate (of course, why start now), it was a few days before my fourth birthday. This is important to the story.

My family and I were about to depart for the airport in our station wagon that had fake wood paneling on the side. In those days, children were not obligated to be strapped into the torture device called a "safety seat." We were allowed to free-roam the vehicle, eventually leaping out the side window in timeless homage to Bo and Luke Duke.

In this particular instance, I was leaning against the back gate of the vehicle, which I had been unable to close securely due to the fact that I was almost four and the door weighed 812 pounds. The scenario that unfolded was not helped by the fact that our driveway was at an incline that resembled the number seven.

Before the car began to back out of the driveway, I leaned on the door—or gravity merely sucked me toward it—and fell face first out of the car. I swiftly smashed down onto my bottom lip or, as my family called it a few moments later, "a plate of gristle."

I was rushed to the emergency room where the doctor took a thorough look at my lip, removing the random parts of driveway that were wedged between cheek and gum. His determination was twofold: I did indeed need stitches, but I was four years old and would therefore chew them out in my sleep. Evidently, lips are the snack standard for sleeping preschoolers.

The bleeding had stopped. The doctor assured that, though extremely unattractive, I would be more than fine. The concern was that the scarring would leave my mouth disfigured or at least the size of Mount Vernon. However, there was nothing that could be done. So my family and I decided to head back toward the airport and celebrate my birthday on vacation anyway.

A vacation on the beach of Jekyll Island. Where my broken mouth could frolic in the painless abandon of the ocean's salt water.

Evidently, the things people own in third-world countries are fairly important to them.

And by things, I don't mean what you and I might call things. You and I might own things like a souvenir Smurf mug or a chess set carved out of the bone marrow of a yak.

In third-world countries, the term "things" refers more to the necessities: The bicycle that takes the owner the twenty miles to work. The sometimes cardboard walls the owner finds shelter between. And these things are quite important to the owner. Not in the status way that our things are important. In the life-or-death way.

In 1991, I lived for six weeks in Timisoara, Romania. This was only a few years after the Wall fell, and the bullet holes of the Revolution had not yet been cemented over in the central square. The bloodstains of the children who had lined up holding hands in front of the tanks to stop them had not been scrubbed away with bleach. The secret rooms in the graveyard where ministers of the Gospel were tortured with hot wax in their bullet wounds had not yet been dismantled. We were one of the first groups to arrive during the first month American groups were allowed inside. And we discovered the hard way that the things people own in third-world countries are fairly important to them—but not very important to us.

THIRD PAUSE
for important autobiographical information

I had never realized of what little importance the things I own are to me until I was robbed. Or, I should say, until I was robbed twice.

In early autumn of 2003, I was away from home for one of the more excruciating weeks of my work year—a job that I could not choose to return from early without serious financial ramifications. It always seemed to be during this particular week of the year that things would happen back at home in my absence—things that I needed to be there for:

- *My wife falling ill.*
- *My daughter's first time as a flower girl.*
- *My son's head splitting open and needing stitches.*

These are pivotal moments for a father, but even more so for a family.

They need their husbands and daddies at these crucial moments. To hold them. To reassure. But this was always the one week that I could not quickly return.

And this was the unfortunate week that the carnies invaded my home.

It was never actually proven that it was the employees of the carnival, but the rash of break-ins that smothered Tulsa, Oklahoma, over the course of that two-week period mapped out a perfect circle around the fairgrounds and came to an abrupt halt when their caravan drove out of town. Also, neighbors reported that the getaway car was selling corndogs.

The robbery scenario would actually seem funnier if it had not first been discovered by my six-year-old daughter Morgan, who had, before that moment, not yet been introduced to the feeling of an unsafe home. Kaysie drove up the driveway and was perplexed to find that the clothing that had been in her closet was now strewn across the yard. She thought perhaps I had returned home early and was pulling another unfunny joke. Kaysie was on the cell phone with her mother when she approached the front door (which was already open) and saw what had once appeared to be our living room. Electronic equipment was now ripped from the entertainment system, cords hanging askew, clothes and rummaged remains everywhere, mud tracks throughout the carpet. Kaysie wasn't sure what was going on.

But in her spirit, Morgan was certain. She began to cry and wail, "I want my Daddy," as Kaysie spoke into the phone repeatedly, "Someone has been here!" and her mother yelled back, "Get out of the house! Get out of the house now!" Kaysie hurried the kids back into the car and drove away quickly to a friend's house nearby where she was able to contact the police.

I, on the other hand, was in the throes of my job a state away. I had been up almost all night for several days straight when my cell phone rang. On the other end was my friend, Matt. He uttered two of my least favorite words.

"Don't panic."

And, of course, I did. Because why would anyone tell you not to panic unless those words were about to be followed by information that would, without the qualifier, be certain to make one panic? Matt explained to me that the police had just burrowed into our home with drawn weapons only to discover that whomever had been there was now gone, but that they had kicked in the back door, destroying part of the kitchen wall. They had also vandalized our bedroom, ruining some personal items like the children's birth certificates. Many items had been stolen, including my wife's wedding ring and our checkbook. But the thieves had not only taken. They had left something behind: a seed of fear that was now being watered inside of my family.

So don't panic.

I tried to find a way to resolve the job quickly and get home. I had a need to console my wife and kids. I had a need to be there, to see the damage, to have a thief's face to direct my anger toward. But there was no way out. Not without substantial damage to my company's reputation in business. As painful as it was to stay, it would be worse to enter the season of fixing the damage with even more working against us. So my wife pulled away from the police to speak to me on the phone. She hid herself in the closet for privacy, and we cried. She felt that her home had been stolen—not a house or things—but a sense of belonging. And she wanted it back.

When I did return home a few days later, it was clear to me just how much a part of God's plan the Church is when it behaves properly. And by that statement, I refer to the people in the Church. They had rallied around our family, temporarily repairing what had been broken, immediately cleaning, taking care of our children, bringing meals, even

*flash*BANG

sleeping over to make Kaysie feel safe. Love quickly invaded our home with a greater ferocity than fear had and swiftly drove it out. We rallied together as a family, prayed, embraced, and listened as our children described the happenings to me in great detail, reliving what was now an enormous adventure and omitting the scary parts.

Our family began to slowly heal with a bit of paranoia mixed in as the week soon dissolved into our normal crazy schedule. One week to the day after the house break-in, I was at the office, and Kaysie was at Morgan's ballet practice. As Kaysie sat inside, a woman came running into the lobby.

WOMAN: *Does anyone here own a blue van?*
KAYSIE: I own a blue van.
WOMAN: *You've just been robbed.*

(An elongated moment of stunned silence.)

KAYSIE: NO WAY!

The admittedly ridiculous truth was—we HAD been robbed. Again. Twice. In one week. Kaysie ventured out into the parking lot to discover that—in a completely filled lot of cars with ours smack in the random middle—OUR van had indeed been burglarized—the only vehicle in the entire parking lot, in fact, to be burglarized. The driver's window had been smashed in, and Kaysie's purse had been stolen.

For those keeping score, that's two stolen checkbooks in one week. For those who have never experienced this unfortunate coincidence, allow me to paint the picture accurately.

1. *Realize first checkbook is stolen.*
2. *Cancel first checking account.*
3. *Cancel first savings account.*

4. *Freeze all finances to make certain no checks were forged before accounts cancelled.*
5. *Contact Social Security for potential identity fraud.*
6. *Unfreeze finances.*
7. *Open new checking and savings accounts.*
8. *Receive new book of checks.*
9. *Have second checkbook stolen.*
10. *Realize second checkbook is stolen.*
11. *Return to cancel second checking account.*
12. *Return to cancel second savings account.*
13. *Freeze all finances again.*
14. *Recontact Social Security to watch for second, separate potential identity fraud.*
15. *Attempt to unfreeze finances.*
16. *Be accused of money laundering by bank.*

Because as difficult as it was for us to believe this story was actually happening, it was even more difficult for the bank to believe. In fact, they did not. They suspected foul play on our part. This required several follow-up items on the to-do list:

17. *Weep uncontrollably in front of bank representative.*
18. *Visit City of Tulsa main office to receive Police Report numbers.*
19. *Discover Police Report numbers are not available as insurance adjusters are taking their sweet time.*
20. *Call insurance to encourage finishing of claim.*
21. *Return to City of Tulsa main office to receive Police Report numbers.*
22. *Take numbers to bank.*
23. *Revel as bank regretfully believes us.*
24. *Scream "In your face, Communists!" at all bank employees.*
25. *Open new checking and savings accounts.*

A full month later, we were finally aware of how much money was in our bank accounts and were able to move along, returning to ordinary life. We were grateful that our family was safe, our home was resuming normalcy, and that the only real loss was the minor one we referred to as our possessions.

Wait just a second.

OUR POSSESSIONS?!

Suddenly, the truth began to germinate. My leather jacket! My video camera! My 35mm still-photo camera! MY XBOX! All gone! All of the creature comforts at the end of the day dissipated into smoke only to be replaced by something worth 60 percent of the original item's value because, evidently, we just don't seem to pay our insurance company enough on the months that nothing is stolen to merit them replacing every bit of what we have lost when the time comes.

Now, I was truly irate. Not only did the robber in question invade my privacy and my safety—he invaded my PLEASURE! My possessions. The things that I possess or perhaps possess me had been erased in this tragedy, this crime.

And that, indeed, made me very, very angry.

Upon landing on the tarmac in Timisoara in an airplane built by Tarom Romanian airlines, I knew our team was in for an uphill battle. We were fourteen members strong, including myself, my brother Dav, eight women, and a nine-foot-tall German theology major named Claus—pronounced like the Nazi, not the Santa. Each of us brought two pieces of luggage for our six-week stay. This, of course, equals twenty-eight bags.

Only four of them made it to Romania on that plane.

The next plane would arrive in seven days. It would take an additional three days beyond those to negotiate our clothing back. That gave me ten days to wear the one outfit I was currently wearing: a wool suit. It was 102 degrees outside. It was going to be a fun week.

Little did I know at the time that regardless of how difficult Romania made things on us, we were going to accidentally make it a whole lot harder on them. The loss of our own things created an unfortunate necessity. We, a team of clumsy Americans, would be obliged to borrow their things. This would not seem to be a problem unless one considers the fact that Westerners only assume that they actually take care of the things they utilize. I can personally attest to the reality that we, in fact, do not use much care at all.

The joy began the very first day when our hosts invited us into town with them. Though I was wearing a thick suit, I agreed that our team would accompany them, ignorant to the fact that we were all going to hike four miles, and that it was about to rain very hard. I remain finely attuned even now, thirteen years later, to the precise scent of six parts wool, two parts rain, two parts human flop sweat. This was the good news.

The bad news, which I did not discover until I was wringing out my necktie by hand, was that I was going to be preaching the service that evening—or in layman's terms, in eighteen minutes.

To make a long story short, the evening went very well from a ministry standpoint while going very poorly from the vantage of my own comfort. Cold moist wool chafes absolutely everywhere, but God fell in the midst of it, and many were healed, restored, and affected in powerful and spiritual ways. I chalked it up as lesson number 1: I don't need to have everything go my way in order for things to go God's way. I don't need to feel right for Him to move.

The primary problem with lessons numbered "1" is that they are quickly swept aside and forgotten. This is what makes rules numbered "2" through "317" necessary—and unfortunately all of these lessons in Romania were at least partially named "Claus."

Claus was a clumsy German. And tactless. Trust me, these are understatements. And I can say this now in good conscience because

Claus is currently a very mature and godly leader, living permanently as a missionary abroad. But he was not mature and leader-like in Romania. In Romania, he was learning—or, more accurately, refusing to learn or change or keep his mouth shut or just for one second not BREAK SOMETHING IMPORTANT!

Again, the things that are important to Romanians are not always the things that are important to Americans because we are petty and born with a sense of entitlement—but I believe it is safe to say that the "things" Claus had a hand in breaking were, indeed, important on a worldwide scale. Claus broke the sorts of things that instigate international conflicts.

There were six things broken in all. And the list reads like a frightening children's book.

THINGS BROKEN

I. The chair.

Claus broke a chair by leaning back on its hind legs.

This is not uncommon unless you consider three important and applicable facts:

1. The chair was two feet tall.
2. Claus was seven feet tall.
3. Claus was warned.

This *bothered* the Romanian family.

We were no longer allowed to sit.

2. The washing machine.

Claus broke the washing machine by leaving something sharp in his pocket.

This is not uncommon unless you consider three equally important facts:

1. The washing machine was Romanian and had exposed thin rubber hoses that could be ripped on the inside.
2. The entire team was warned and required to pull the pockets of their clothing inside-out for this very purpose.
3. Claus' clothes had to go through a security inspection stage before being placed in the washing machine due to the incident with the chair.

It was never actually proven that the sharp object had been in the pocket of Claus—but, deep down, I knew it had to be him because Claus sneaked a pair of shorts in past the checkpoint. He didn't check the pockets. He didn't think it should be that big a deal to wash his clothes.

This *agitated* the Romanian family.
We were no longer allowed to wash.

3. The van.

A petite girl on our team rested her feet on the dashboard of the rental van from Germany. The moment she touched the windshield with her toe, the glass suddenly splintered into shrapnel.

This may not *directly* be Claus' fault, but I regard this as his responsibility for three reasons:

1. He was staring at the windshield intensely when it shattered.
2. The breaking of the windshield (being an accident) would not have been a big deal without the two previous breakings.
3. The van and Claus were both German.

This prompted *fury* from all surrounding Romanians.
We were no longer allowed to ride in automobiles.

4. The contact.

Claus broke the heart of the contact in the city of Baia Mare while Claus, the contact, and I were canoeing together on a lake. The conversation went something like this. Keep in mind that the contact was sitting eight inches away from Claus and that the contact was the pastor of the local church.

CLAUS:	*I don't like this city as much as the other cities.*
ME:	Claus?
CLAUS:	*Don't take that the wrong way. All I mean is: of all the cities we've been in, I like this one the least.*
ME:	Stop talking.
CLAUS:	*It's not that I hate it—well, okay. Yeah. I hate it.*
ME:	CLAUS!
CLAUS:	*Oh, no, no, no. Don't misunderstand me. It's not that it isn't pretty. It's beautiful.*
ME:	Oh. Okay.
CLAUS:	*It's the people I don't like.*
ME:	CLAUUUUUUUUUS!
CLAUS:	*Well, not all the people. Just the people in the church.*
ME:	You can go back to America now.
CLAUS:	*Mainly this guy in the boat.*

But all four of these destructions pale in comparison to the queen mother of items destroyed. The most unbelievable belonging we undid was so large that it literally changed the life of eight Romanian families. And not for the better.

Inconceivable.
Implausible.
This can't be right.

So went the responses from doctors when they re-examined my bottom lip a week after the accident. The expectation had, of course, been at least a little scarring, if not slight facial disfigurement.

Instead, my bottom lip looked exactly like a bottom lip.

The expansive time my four-year-old mouth spent in the salty ocean had cinched the wounds up and caused them to heal at a remarkable rate. The concern the doctor had that I would bite at my stitches is actually what helped form them back into the shape of a lip. My chewing on them helped mold them back as they healed.

The most remarkable aspect of all is that—while having the appearance of a lip—the lip is, in fact, a large lump of scar tissue. It is thick and calloused. If you were to pull my bottom lip away from my teeth, to this day, you would feel a mountain of lumps and scars. There is no shortage of evidence that my accident took place. But, for some heavenly purpose, all of that proof is hidden on the inside of my mouth, where it goes unnoticed without further inspection.

Well—not completely unnoticed. After all, my lip is currently 65 percent larger than your average bottom lip. If writing doesn't work out, I could always become a spokesperson for collagen injections.

We actually felt like we were on an upswing. In the streets of Timisoara, ministry was beginning to bear fruit. We were seeing hardened hearts return time and time again to hear us speak about our spiritual experiences, and we were seeing hearts soften and lives changed. These were not quick and easy fixes. These people wanted to know first that we meant business. That we were living what we were saying. That we had learned our lesson and were not going to carelessly destroy the things that matter to them anymore.

We were on the drive to lunch after one such successful ministry day when a gypsy woman physically stopped our van at an intersection. She began screaming into the driver's window in her mother tongue. Our translator kept saying, "Slow down. You aren't making any sense." Finally, the translator turned to us and said, "I don't understand her." I replied, "Well, what does it sound like she is saying?" "She asked if we were the Americans, and when I said we were, she kept repeating the strangest thing.

She keeps saying we drowned her home."

Faucets in Eastern Europe are a funny thing, of course. So funny, in fact, that upon arriving at our Romanian apartment at the beginning of our trip, we were all given a crash course—a verbal lecture—on the proper way to turn the faucets on and off. In America, to turn a faucet on, you turn clockwise. In Eastern Europe, it is, of course, the opposite. This evidently has something to do with Parliament and the position of the equator and is very confusing. Nonetheless, a rule was set that I—the team leader—would go to every sink before departure each morning and turn all of the sinks off. That way, there would be no confusion.

And no one to blame but myself.

The particular day in question, the city's water had been cut off by the government in the middle of the night. I watched as different team members fiddled with the faucets in vain. I took note that I would need to make certain everyone had exited the building before I turned the faucets off correctly, then lock up immediately behind me. This is what I did, and I was certain—CERTAIN—that I had turned every faucet securely clockwise, then locked up the apartment. This new gypsy woman's news was disconcerting. We immediately sped back to defend our innocence.

When we approached the apartment building, we knew something was amiss because most every resident of the building was standing in the street threateningly slapping a bat and/or chain against their open palm. I hurried inside to discover literally inches of water gathered all about our apartment. Every single faucet was turned on full blast—hot water—and the flooding and steam had ruined flooring, walls, paint, carpeting—but had not stopped there.

You see, our residence was on the third floor with one apartment to our right and another to our left, leaving us in the corner. The flooding was so severe that it literally destroyed not merely our apartment and the two beside, but also the three beneath on floor two AND the three beneath on floor one. In other words, the fifth belonging our team destroyed was ...

5. Nine apartments.

This would be bad news in the Hamptons. In Timisoara, Romania, it was a burgeoning international crisis. The Wall had fallen. A group of fourteen American Christians were allowed inside. And now, their bacchanalia of water-wasting had rendered eight Romanian families homeless. We were now slightly less popular than Adolf Hitler.

It was our responsibility to pay for all of the damages. So I looked into our team fund, which I had managed with frugality. We were able to foot the bill for all nine apartments and still have forty dollars left. Of course, there were still three weeks left in the trip to feed fourteen people. After a lengthy day of reparation on every level, we finally shut the door, and I retreated head-in-hands to my bedroom to soak in my own inadequacy.

It was perhaps an hour later when Claus appeared.

CLAUS:	*Mark?*
MARK:	Not right now.
CLAUS:	*Okay. It's a funny thing, though.*
MARK:	What's a funny thing?
CLAUS:	*You know how you told us that you would turn all the faucets off every morning?*

My eyebrows began to smoke.

MARK: Claus, why do I not think this is going to be a funny thing?

CLAUS: *Well—I was pretty sure that you had turned them all the wrong direction, so I used the other key, came in after you left, and turned every faucet in the apartment full blast the other way.*

I believe, at this moment, I could actually taste my own blood.

CLAUS: *Isn't that a funny thing?*

From this point on, every moment of every day felt like an eggshell dance. We were doing our best to focus on ministry while simultaneously keeping our eyes in the corner of our sockets to avoid anything we might potentially damage. The other thirteen members of the team were assigned perpetual Claus watch—meaning he was never to be left alone—and we were to remain alert, watching out for swift flailing clumsiness on his part. Any spastic Claus motion was to trigger the immediate sound of a whistle blow, to which all thirteen on the team were required to dogpile Claus, regardless of what we were doing or how far we might be from him at the time.

This seemed foolproof, and, as the final weeks progressed, we matured with much success, connecting with the church and community. We eventually earned back the right to sit in chairs, wash our clothes, and ride in moving vehicles. The eight Romanian families in question were enjoying newly renovated homes. Our bad fortune seemed to have dissipated.

Until it was time to leave.

Did I say we were robbed twice?

I meant to say that we were robbed three times. I failed to mention the robbery by the insurance company.

The agent (as insurance people are called so that they can pretend they are spies) arrived and was immediately genial with a detached air of "been there, paid for that." Dealing with victims of robbery was so old hat to him that nothing we had to say phased him. This is not his fault—he was merely doing his job—but we NEEDED a "representative." Someone to see the busted doorjamb and, on the line next to its question of worth, state the words—

> *How do you place a price tag on fear entering a home,*
> *on dignity being smeared on the carpet like so much*
> *backyard mud from a stolen sneaker? How do you give*
> *financial compensation that equals the destruction of a*
> *family's haven? The dinner table where they gathered for*
> *meals and prayers was now splattered with the debris of*
> *a broken-down back door. How can that be paid back?*

But, of course, instead, he took the lowest estimate for repair and reduced it by 40 percent. He had to. It was his job. He had done it a thousand times. Witnessed the aftermath of a thousand injustices. Stopped empathizing somewhere in the middle of that thousand. And reduced our remedy to a mathematic formula that would heal our wallet by 60 percent and grant the agent free movie tickets if our evaluation of his time with us was at least eight stars out of ten.

In his hurry to evaluate, he wasn't healing at all. He wasn't hearing. He had a formula. A device. The same method of fixing for everyone he encountered with no variation. He smiled and paused for emotion because the agent handbook said so. But we were not moved. We accepted the check. We had resigned ourselves to the fact that it was the best recompense available. But the entire experience left a knot of disillusionment in our stomachs. Because, for weeks, we had struggled with having no face to place on the invisible invader of our home and, therefore, lived with a latent hopelessness. And, as hard as I tried for it not to be so, that intruder now had a very specific face.

*flash*BANG

And that face looked very much like the face of our insurance agent.

Six weeks had come and gone. Ministry had been completed. It was now time to reassess what had been done and bond together as a group. I had orchestrated an entire open afternoon in our schedule to debrief as a team and celebrate—to give our team of fourteen what every family needs after a challenging ordeal: closure. A time to genuinely say goodbye. We only had one errand left before we could begin: we had to go to the travel agency and—for the fifth time in six weeks—reconfirm our flight. A pleasant female travel agent (*there's that word again*) helped me confirm the details.

> WOMAN: *That's fourteen passengers all the way through to Chicago, Mr. Steele.*
> MARK: Thank you so much. You've been a great help.
> WOMAN: *One other thing, though.*
> MARK: What's that?
> WOMAN: *You've waited awfully late to purchase your four tickets to Bucharest.*

Throughout history, there are many statements that have been labeled as "haunting," depending on the person to which the statements are made. Three of the most haunting statements are, of course:

- "How about a night at the theater instead, President Lincoln?"
- "Get a little closer to that iceberg, Captain."
- "I think you should propose to Jennifer Lopez."

But, slightly lesser-known is the ominous phrase: "You've waited awfully late to purchase your four tickets to Bucharest."

> MARK: What four tickets to Bucharest?
> WOMAN: *You do realize that four members of your team do*

	not depart from Timisoara. They depart
	tomorrow from Bucharest.
MARK:	What do you mean depart from Bucharest?
WOMAN:	*Did the American travel agent not inform you of*
	this? You must arrange for these four to get to
	Bucharest immediately, or they will be unable to
	return home.
MARK:	What do you mean immediately?
WOMAN:	***If you buy the tickets right now, they will have to***
	get on that plane in three hours.

And that did it. Devastation. We would be completely out of cash. Four members of our team—two girls, Claus' roommate Jared, and my brother Dav—would not be allowed to debrief or say goodbye to six weeks' worth of relationships with the church and contacts. We would not be able to relax. Instead, we would have to purchase the tickets, hurry back to the apartment, and pack hastily. It would then be time to hurry once again to the airport and see Dav and the others off to the terminal in Bucharest. Once there, they would be required to sleep in the locked airport overnight in order to make the flight the next morning that would, ironically, lay over in Timisoara—where we would then join them. Due to Romanian law, it was impossible for them to simply begin the trip at the layover.

In a hurricane of activity, our plan succeeded, and the remaining ten of us found ourselves back in our apartment at midnight—exhausted and emotionally spent—but still needing to pack. As I sat in my bedroom, filling my suitcase, Claus entered. At that moment, he began the conversation that would—before the evening ran out—break the only thing remaining to be broken.

6. My spirit.

CLAUS:	(laughing)
MARK:	Why are you laughing?
CLAUS:	*A funny thing.*

MARK:	NO! No more funny things. You are banned from all funny things. Forever. Or at least until I don't know you anymore.
CLAUS:	*Okay.*
MARK:	You're still smiling.
CLAUS:	*It's still a funny thing.*
MARK:	Will I regret asking you?
CLAUS:	*No. It's not really a big deal.*
MARK:	Will you leave my room if I ask you?
CLAUS:	*Okay.*
MARK:	What is this funny thing?
CLAUS:	*I can't find my passport.*

Not a funny thing. No. This is not a funny thing. And I know funny things. Milk flowing uncontrollably out of one or both nostrils. This is funny. A man in a bee costume bursting through a drywall while yelling in Spanish. Margaret Thatcher performing lambada: the forbidden dance. Funny. But to be in Eastern Europe? To have angered families and pastors and government officials? To be six hours from leaving for the airport and Claus has lost his passport?

Not funny.

MARK:	WHEN DID YOU SEE IT LAST?!
CLAUS:	*You're yelling.*
MARK:	I ALWAYS YELL AT FUNNY THINGS!
CLAUS:	I *saw it not too long ago. In Brasov.*
MARK:	(silence)
CLAUS:	*Why are you not saying anything?*
MARK:	We were in Brasov two weeks ago.
CLAUS:	*Yeah. It was in my lap, I think. At some restaurant. No—wait. I saw it in my room here since then. Maybe. I'm not too good with details.*
MARK:	Claus.
CLAUS:	*Your face is turning purple.*

MARK:	That's what a heart attack does to the face. Do you know what I need for you to do?
CLAUS:	*No. I don't.*
MARK:	I need for you to go BACK TO YOUR ROOM and NOT COME OUT until you have FOUND YOUR PASSPORT!
CLAUS:	*Right now?*
MARK:	YES!
CLAUS:	*But—I'm sleepy.*
MARK:	**CLAUUUUUUUUUS!**

At this point, the word "Claus" was becoming a profanity of sorts. I was livid. So Claus retreated to his room where he found all sorts of interesting doodles in his notebook, but no official papers of any kind. Over the next two hours, Claus had short, fraudulent epiphanies that he had left his passport at the following locations with the following consequences:

1. **THE GIRLS' HOUSE.** Upon phoning them with the news, the girls on our team spent the next two hours unpacking and uncleaning absolutely everything they had packed and cleaned in order to discover that the passport had actually never been in their home.

2. **THE CONTACT'S HOUSE.** Upon receiving the news by phone, the contact's family stayed up into the wee hours dismantling everything they owned, thereby breaking many new things—all in order to discover that the passport was not there either.

3. **THE HOST CHURCH.** As no one stayed overnight at the church, two of the guys on our team RAN the twenty-five minutes to the church, BROKE IN, and RUMMAGED through everything in the building to discover that—no—the passport was also not there.

flash BANG

The remaining few of us overturned every belonging in the men's apartment. The only bag, in fact, that I discovered intact and still packed was Claus' bag sitting neatly on his bed.

MARK: Why haven't you dumped this out?
CLAUS: *I just packed it. Why would I want to mess it up?*

So, I messed Claus' bag up for him—taking great joy in doing so. I took one item out of the bag at a time, checking it thoroughly and hurling it across the room and, in several cases, "accidentally" out the window—but alas, there was not a passport to be found. It seemed that Claus had, in fact, managed to misplace the passport somewhere that could not be checked overnight.

CLAUS: *Oh well. Can't find it. I'm going to bed.*
MARK: You're going to what?
CLAUS: *Bed. I'm so tired.*
MARK: You do realize that you are making my brain
            seep out of my ears.
CLAUS: *For crying out loud, just chill out and let me
            sleep.*
MARK: How can you possibly go to sleep?!
            Without your passport, you can't leave tomorrow!
CLAUS: *Come on, Mark. They don't take it that seriously.*

You know the part of the cartoon where the character's head turns into a very loud train whistle, and then his body actually explodes into liftoff like a rocket with a fuse. Then, upon leaving the atmosphere, the cartoon character actually erupts into fireworks?

I didn't take this quite that well.

MARK: *CLAUUUUUUUUUUS!*
            THIS IS NOT AN ISSUE OF THE MOOD
            OF THE PEOPLE AT ROMANIAN SECURITY!

THEY DON'T SELECT WHO GOES OR STAYS
VIA PAPER, ROCK, SCISSORS! IT IS **LAW**!
PURE COMMUNIST EUROPEAN LAW! NO
PASSPORT—NO CLUMSY GERMAN MAN
GOING HOME! THAT IS NOT OPINION! IT
IS **FACT**! LIKE THE **FACT** THAT
WINDSHIELDS BREAK AND THE **FACT**
THAT ROMANIAN PASTORS HAVE
FEELINGS AND THE **FACT** THAT FAUCETS
IN EUROPE TURN OFF **CLOCKWISE**!

I'm not certain if my incessant screaming at three in the morning caused some slumbering synapse to fire inside Claus' brain, or if he merely began to actually engage in the passport hunt—but for some reason, amid my lunatic ravings, Claus had a personal epiphany.

CLAUS:	*I GOT IT!*
MARK:	You got it?! You found it?!
CLAUS:	*No. Not "I found it." I got it! I figured out where my passport is.*
MARK:	REEEEALLY?! Where?
CLAUS:	*I must have accidentally put it in Jared's bag.*

Let's review, shall we?

Jared was one of the four teammates who, earlier that same day, needed to hurry to Bucharest, the capital of Romania. He was presently locked in the airport two hours away with no means of communication. He would not be allowed to get off the plane in Timisoara, and we would not be able to get on to retrieve the passport from his bag, because odds are, it would be checked luggage. In other words: it was the worst possible place the passport could have been.

I contacted the host pastor immediately, and a plan was devised. The church had a contact who lived approximately one hour from the Bucharest airport. He would be wakened by phone to drive to the airport with a few minister friends. At that point, they would run to every window and door in the building, banging loudly until someone, anyone responded. That someone who responded would then be asked to find the four Americans in order to communicate the need to rummage through their luggage. If the passport was found, a negotiation would then be made with cash to smuggle the passport off the plane in Timisoara by aid of a flight attendant, who would then get it into the hands of Claus in the airport. Within a half-hour, the plan was in action. It was now almost four. We would leave at seven. It was our only hope.

Having had his first epiphany in twenty years, Claus was completely exhausted and begged to be allowed to sleep. I resolved to permit this, but with the one condition that if, in fact, his passport failed to be in Jared's bag, Claus would be learning a new permanent language.

Claus responded with the double-edged politeness of "thanks—finally" and retreated to his bed.

I was undone. I could not sleep, so I stepped out onto the porch awning. Deeply troubled, I attempted to process what had gone wrong. The team had made such a fine comeback. We had won the Romanian people back over after offending and hurting them so badly with our destruction. We had bonded as a team. I had gone this far and not exploded. And then tonight. Tonight. Tonight. Tonight. How did this one evening, this one incident, seem to undo all that we had worked so hard to accomplish?

I began to pray, attempting to find the answers amidst my confusion and hurt. If we had fulfilled God's plan, why did I feel so badly now, at the end. I gave this thought to God in an act of desperation. Why me? Why this? Why Claus? I turned around, to walk back into the apartment. This is when I found him, standing in the doorway, with that sheepish smirk on his face.

MARK:	What is it now?
CLAUS:	*A funny thing.*
MARK:	(silence)
CLAUS:	*I found it?*

The question mark at the end of what would otherwise have been a statement from Claus led me to believe that, though I would appreciate the result, I would not actually like the details of what he had to say.

MARK:	Where.	Was.	It?
CLAUS:	*Well—*		
MARK:	Claus—where did you find the passport?		
CLAUS:	*When I lay down to go to sleep, I moved my bag over, and it was there—sitting on the bed, underneath my suitcase. I forgot that I had been looking at it earlier tonight. It was in my room the entire time.*		
MARK:	Why is that a funny thing?		
CLAUS:	*Because if you had just listened to God and let me go to sleep the first time I said I wanted to, none of this would have happened!*		

I spent the next hour attempting to reach the contact (or anyone, for that matter) by phone to stop the expedition to the Bucharest airport. But, all I received were busy signals. Everyone in ministry in Romania was awake and on the phone—searching for a single German passport that had always been nestled snugly in the owner's bed.

We departed the next morning after bidding farewell to a Romanian ministry staff that was exhausted and at the end of its rope. They loved us. They would miss us. They wished us well. But they were very, very glad we were flying away in the opposite direction.

As I watched the land disappear from the window of the plane, I began to realize that I was leaving Romania with much more inside of me than when I had arrived. But I began to wonder: At what expense did our betterment come? Had we fulfilled our reason for traveling so far: to indeed bless these people? Or had we taken much, much more than we had returned?

Was it possible that, in my eyes, the ministry had succeeded—but in the eyes of those we had come to reach, a robbery had taken place?

Perhaps a robbery did, indeed, take place. And perhaps it was not our team who was robbed. Perhaps it was our team who did the robbing.

In our attempt to bring the truth to the hurting, we had made the fatal flashbang mistake. We had assumed that bringing the truth mattered so much that nothing else we did would matter at all.

In our hurry to evaluate, we weren't healing anyone. We weren't hearing. We had a formula. A device. The same method of fixing for everyone we encountered with no variation. We smiled and paused for emotion because the ministry handbook said so. But we were not moved.

Well, no, that isn't exactly true. We were moved. We made lifelong relationships. We felt for them. But we were not moved enough for our habits to change.

I had a heart for the people. A heart for ministry. But somewhere in the middle of six weeks, I stopped allowing their plight inside my heart, and I, instead, began playing the part of the insurance agent. As I witnessed the hardships and grew closer to those around us, I realized that things were about to break. Things inside of me that had been cold and selfish. Dams and devices that held in passion and kept me proper. But just as the cracks were forming inside, I made an unconscious decision.

The decision to do it all myself. To reach these people my way. In my strength. Within my experience. And, without knowing it, the spackle inside of me began covering the cracks, sealing the bricks, and keeping those walls from falling.

The problem is: when cultures clash, something is bound to break. And with the reinforcements growing within ourselves, the only breakables left were on their side.

We broke their things. We broke their trust. We broke their confidence. We broke their belief that we had come, in fact, to be broken. And, in that process, as the first team of Americans to arrive, though we brought and did many wonderful things—we left the remnants of a robbery behind us.

It was not until a decade or so later that I realized that the destructive decision came at the very beginning, when the plane first arrived. We saw their faces. Heard their stories. Lived in their world. At that moment, a decision was made. A decision to view our job there as one of two things:

> *1. An opportunity to make their problems our problems.*
> *2. An opportunity to allow their problems to only affect us temporarily.*

We had inexplicably chosen the latter. In the end, there was much noise made. Great clang and clatter and billowing clouds of smoke. But it was only a flashbang. Because we did not leave a crater of love. You can't set off a true explosion if you are afraid to get caught in the blast. We, instead, left behind splinters of a chair, remnants of a washing machine, and water stains where there used to be homes. Nothing that said, "Jesus." Only things that said, "America."

When our own home was burglarized twelve years later, we needed someone else's heart to break for us more than we needed our broken things fixed. A decade certainly has a way of putting you in the other guy's shoes. Just like Morgan, we saw our broken world and cried aloud, "I want my Daddy." We found Him in the members of our church. We did not find Him in our insurance agent because you don't go to the heart that's hardened if you need the blood inside. The people of Timisoara had looked for their Daddy inside of us and found, instead, souls who wavered between what should be done and what would get us in and out safely. We were, at times, the Church, and at others, the insurance agent. Somehow, the mixture of the holy and the human smelled too much of the latter. We wanted to mend their brokenness, but we were afraid to break.

Because breaking can cause scar tissue. Breaking may not heal back with the same appearance.

Breaking.
Tearing.
Falling face first.

It could make the face somehow different—somehow less than it had been before. It was plausible that being the thing that was broken in order for others to be healed would change us forever—in a way with which I was uncomfortable.

It was plausible because I felt I would be broken for the people, but I would be required to heal myself.

And in my lack of understanding, it seemed most logical at the time that there would be no way to come back from brokenness with greater strength.

Unless ...

... Unless I would not be required to do the healing myself at all.

I would only be required to run into the ocean and play in the healing salts.

That, somehow, in an action that caused me to forget my wounds completely, they would be most prone to healing. That in the obedience of hurting and bleeding for someone outside myself, a special grace would be placed upon the new gaping holes in my soul.

That, somehow, outside of logic and reason, my very teeth could chew and mold away at the damage inside my mouth, smoothing the scars by grace back into shape.

The shape of what they were originally meant to be, only with greater strength to endure future breaking.

Those scars would lead me to a place greater than I had been before them due to the combination of three powerful forces:

The sacrifice of being broken.
The healing of His grace.
And the results of my own teethmarks.

unwrapping
THE ATTACK OF LOVE

The truth is: we don't like to see brokenness in others any more than we like to be broken ourselves. We don't like to dig that far into another's life. We would prefer not to sink our teeth in due to the aftertaste of a life in need.

And let's face it. In this day and age, our own lives are so screwed up, who has time to help sort out anyone else's? Even Christian lives are often lived every-man-for-himself because there is so little time to get our own house in order. Certainly, we don't actually SAY this. We say that outreach and missions and caring for our fellow man are some of the most important and often-implemented aspects of our lives. But, is this accurate? Do we actually attempt to look after the next guy as much as or more than the one standing in our shoes? No. We don't. Because we have told ourselves that it would be tragic to affect so many other lives for the better only for our own to end in disaster. To this end, until our own lives feel finished, we hesitate to aid in the completion of someone else.

So we bite hesitantly. We test the waters of relationships. We ease in to minimize discomfort. Therefore, our ministry is safe. We truly affect people, but only those who won't rattle our daily lives if the affecting doesn't change them. We open our mouth as if to chomp down hard but, at the last moment, settle for pre-chewed food. We outreach for our own sake and need—not looking for the neediest recipient but instead searching for the guilt-resolve that fits best within our schedule. There is an inherent problem with this sort of unreach.

Our jaws are rotting from lack of exercise because we are not leaving teethmarks.

Teethmarks. Biting down hard and leaving behind something

uncomfortable. Something that causes a blemish and an audible ouch. Something that awakens—that draws blood. Something aggressive that changes and lasts. Not a flashbang, but rather a crater of care.

Now, I may not always behave as if I believe in teethmarks. I may behave as if I believe that reaching out is supposed to be an open hand allowing the hurting party to do all the grabbing. That once I am fixed, all the pain should stop. Unfortunately for me, there is someone who disagrees. His name is Jesus.

Jesus hears news that a friend of His is dead. And He weeps. But He doesn't weep because the friend is dead. He weeps because the women who told Him His friend is dead have chosen to believe this. They have determined that Lazarus is a lost cause.

To be fair, death is the sort of thing that we tend to view as final. Regardless of your theology, good people die because there is a better healing after that suffering. But Jesus was troubled. Not because the women believed death was real, but because they had not really listened to Him.

He had made it clear two days ago: "Lazarus' sickness will not end in death." He was God—death's superior— and He had made an executive decision in the case of Lazarus. The result of his malady would bring glory to God.

But Lazarus' sisters, Mary and Martha, had only believed Jesus to a point. They had, indeed, believed that Jesus would not allow Lazarus to die. But they misunderstood—thinking there was a depth Lazarus could drown where Jesus would be unable to dive in after him. The women's faith and minds had limits. In their imagination, Jesus was stronger than the last straw, but once that last straw disappeared, they believed the contest to be lost.

And, right about now, Mary and Martha were having a difficult time with Jesus because He was not returning to stop death from seizing their brother. After all, it had been a promise. Doesn't God's promise mean that He will resolve our issue the exact way we think He should? Well—perhaps not. But, there are clearly only so many conceivable ways this sort of a miracle could be provided, and none of them included Jesus staying put several cities away.

So, from their perspective, Jesus delayed, and Lazarus died. The issue appeared closed. The sisters would continue to believe in Jesus as the Son of God with one exception: that He was either unwilling or incapable of keeping that one promise. As a matter of fact, when Jesus did arrive a few days later, Mary came immediately to Him, fell down at His feet, and said, "Lord, if you had been here, my brother would not have died." Sadness, regret, disillusionment, unanswered questions—all wrapped in a single ball of misunderstanding.

What exactly was the misunderstanding? The placement of "The End" on Lazarus' story. Mary and Martha had assumed the end was now. But they didn't have accurate information. Because of this, they had given up on their own brother—even when Jesus had not given up at all.

"Where have you put him?" Jesus asked. And rather than

tell Him, they showed Him that they had sealed Lazarus inside a tomb with a stone. They had not only had enough time to doubt, they had enough time to finalize. Jesus looked on at the sight and made a command.

"Roll the stone aside."

You see that weight you stuck in front of his escape? You see that label you attached to his life? Well, guess what. You get to move it. You and those like you. Roll it away.

The sisters protested, concerned for the smell. But Jesus responded the way—in our unfortunate society—God often has to respond to our surprise at His greatness:

"Didn't I tell you ..."

Then Jesus told Lazarus to come out of the hole in which he had been buried. And Lazarus did. Wrapped up like a mummy and smelling like four days of decay, Lazarus came out. Lazarus was alive.

But this is not where "The End" belongs either. Because God's breath of life into Lazarus was not enough to complete the miracle.

Lazarus was still bound. Bound with the cloth coffin those who loved him decided he now belonged in. They had determined "The End" by dressing him for death. And that is when the most curious thing of all took place.

Jesus, who had the ability to breathe new life into Lazarus' lungs, who could whisk away Lazarus' entrapments with a lilt of His tiniest finger—this Jesus did not choose to take the final action of freeing Lazarus for Himself. Instead, He made another command.

"Unwrap him. And let him go."

Jesus, having every right to fix our messes Himself, decided that the most healing option for all around would be for the doubters to also be the rescuers. For those who had a tendency to apply bandages and chains to also be the ones to occasionally remove them.

Jesus asked the people to unwrap those He resurrected.

And He still does.

It is you and I that God continues to ask to unwrap them. Unwrap those whom I have written off. Those whom I consider lost causes. Unwrap those whom I have had a hand in tying up as well as those whom I haven't. Be willing to bite so hard that the bandages break.

But I would rather chew the soft food and let the hard cases stay in the tombs because I assume they will both smell and taste horrible. This is why my efforts have resulted in moments of spectacular flashes—without truly changing anything.

Because I cannot pick and choose the way I will be used.

It is an issue of real authentic love for each and every person. It should take a sacrifice on many levels to accomplish God's task because this task is supposed to change me, and change does not occur where circumstances are predictable and comfortable.

Consider for a moment the people, relationships, and situations that you have considered dead. God would dare say that they are merely sleeping. But, they are in need of a swift, deep bite. The sort that leaves a permanent indentation.

Are you willing to bare your teeth and be that person? Because it is the first step toward the answer. The answer to why our plan has not been working and how it, perhaps, could. The clue that leads away from hollow fireworks and into healing that is truly remembered. Remembered enough to bring change.

That is, indeed, a volatile place to be. A daring world where not one soul is safe from our attack of love. Where no one can cower in the shadows and bide their time until mummification. Because there are followers of Christ who are not waiting to be asked for help. We, instead, root out the dying and grab their hand before it is even fully outstretched.

And, in that process, do not even realize that we have just been rescued ourselves.

doing impressions
WHY WE MUST MARINATE

So, I'm holding on to the outside of a moving vehicle, clinging to a metal pipe as what appears to be the end of the world swirls in the dank dark clouds directly above me. The temperature has dropped a good twenty-five degrees in about three seconds. It is springtime in Tornado Alley, and I would be radically concerned about the eighteen crew members (most of them, at this point, swearing) being struck by lightning if I weren't currently more focused on the well-being of the one-of-a-kind automobile prototype in front of me or the two Japanese businessmen who brought it all the way from Tokyo to Tulsa. I struggle to find the accurate translation for "we are all going to die" and instead loudly scream, "Twister!"

This is what we call a memorable moment. But the story did not end there. Neither did it begin. The beginning was slightly less impressive, but just as unexpected.

FOURTH PAUSE
for important autobiographical information

As I mentioned in a prior chapter, I am a comic. But, in reality, that is my night job. My day job is in the world of film and video production. I could take ample time attempting to paint this career as something glamorous, but the truth is, people run around and I point a large piece of equipment at them. Well, it's not exactly me who points the camera at them. My production company, Steelehouse (now, isn't that creative?), is filled with people much more talented at that than I am. So, basically, I think of things at which they are to point the large piece of equipment, and then they go point with great artistic ability.

The autumn prior to the storm, our team entered a short film we were particularly proud of into a festival in Seattle, Washington. The piece won its category and attracted the attention of two of the judges: one from Los Angeles, the other from Japan. Little did we know that a major automobile corporation was making timely decisions concerning which production team would produce their new short film promoting a secret, as-of-yet-unreleased vehicle. Even less did we know that the corporation in question was leaving the decision up to a renowned Japanese filmmaker who had just recently been a judge at this festival in Seattle.

Through a surreal series of phone calls, the Japanese gentleman contacted the Los Angeles gentleman who contacted us. Ideas and scripts were exchanged, and, before we knew it, the prototype vehicle was locked away in an unmarked semi-truck behind our Tulsa offices.

Now, why do I even bring this factoid into the proceedings of this story? Should you really care if I had a great career opportunity? Probably not. It's the sort of story one would tell at a party, thinking it the most intriguing anecdote in the world when, actually, the only person interested is the one doing the telling. But, in this case, the story is important because, though it may seem the opposite for a few moments, it is not about the job. The story is about the people. Them and us. And, of course, about the storm that we weathered in each other's company.

We did not pursue this job. We could not have predicted that we would be stuck in the eye of the storm with these individuals. Shirley MacLaine channeling Nostradamus while holding a Magic 8 Ball could not have attempted to predict it. But God could certainly ordain it and move every human chess piece to make the play in His timing. He did. And where we

would consider a life-threatening, property-destroying storm a bad thing,
God wanted to see if there were silent storms that were stronger.

It began with an air of mystery. These strangers jaunting across the globe to our corner were businessmen—from a major automobile corporation. They did not speak English. And we were to meet and impress them, all at the same time. That sort of pressure will cause you to do a great many things you do not wish to do, but first, it will cause you to attempt to change who you are.

Speaking only for myself, the assumption upon meeting someone impressive is that I must become more impressive than I actually am—somehow matching my impression of their impressiveness, which is often an inaccurate impression. Without knowing what the person I am meeting expects, I choose to believe that they will expect more than my reality. So the fictional face is unfortunately put on.

We were told that this filmmaker was the Spielberg of Japan—which either means that he is the best in his country or he is the only Asian-Jewish man in the world. We were told that he and his entourage would be difficult to read. We were told that they would second-guess and doubt our creative decisions and that we would have to carefully watchdog every move that we made for the next five days. The three arrived, and we began our relationship with trepidation and an air of superficiality. I addressed the first of the group, bowing and greeting him with a rousing "Konichiwa!" To which he informed me that he was the mechanic from Los Angeles and that he was Hispanic.

I truly did make my best attempt to seem professional, impressive, unmoved, and stoic for the first twelve minutes, but upon discovering the common language of a love for film and art, the child in each of us surfaced, and we were soon fast friends—well, technically slow friends as it took us each ten minutes to speak a sentence with the help of the interpreter.

The interpreter had a fondness for American girls and steak sandwiches. This was our common ground as I married an American girl and had been in love with several steak sandwiches. He spoke for the Japanese filmmaker throughout the week. In this vein, he began as a mouthpiece, but as the week progressed, his words were his own.

As the week started with rehearsals and meetings, my business partner, Kevin, and I faced a challenge. We did not want to change who we were or the convictions that we held so dear, nor did we want to offend. The Japanese culture is primarily Buddhist or atheist, but we made it a common practice to pray at the top of our shoot days, whether the production was faith-based or entertainment-based. This has never been for the sake of show or impression as much as it has been for the fact that we desperately need God's help, and we believe that if we hesitate to enact what we believe today, we will freeze up when placed in more precarious situations. We decided we would run the question by our Los Angeles contact. After a brief discussion, we made the decision to keep our normal routine of opening prayer, but that our staff would circle up to do so, making it optional for crew or client.

As we sat down for our very first meal with our new friends, I realized how hesitant I was to stop and pray. In spiritual matters, this is always a certain sign to me that I need to do it. So we stopped and prepared to take the moment. Kevin began, and our Los Angeles contact made an attempt to soften the moment.

> KEVIN: *If you don't mind, we're going to stop for a moment and pray.*
>
> CONTACT: Do you ever do that in Japan? Before meals? Pray?
>
> INTERPRETER: No.
>
> KEVIN: *Okay then.*

I began to pray. Not the most passionate prayer of my walk with Christ. Certainly not the most focused. More than likely one of the most conflicted prayers of my adult life. Within the same one-minute prayer, I felt:

1. Grateful for the opportunity.
2. Concerned with the impression I was giving.

3. Ashamed that I was worried about impressions during a prayer.
4. Abandoned to allow our new friends to think whatever they wanted of us.
5. Determined to lift our new friends up to God.
6. Resolved that I should never doubt to pray again.

We prayed for them. We prayed that our relationship would grow strong over the course of the week. We prayed for our steak sandwiches. And we prayed for good weather.

MARK: Amen.
KEVIN: *This is part of our beliefs. We pray before our meals as a means of gratitude. Of thanks.*
INTERPRETER: It is nice.

Over the next two days, we kept an intense shooting schedule on location, on process trailer (the elaborate apparatus that allows the placing of a large amount of shooting equipment on the outside of a moving vehicle), and in rehearsal. Every time we connected with the clients over a meal, we created a greater bond over our love for film and our artistic choices regarding this particular shoot. We were of like mind on the project, and it was a true pleasure.

On Wednesday, we were slightly ahead of schedule and optimistic because the weather forecast gave a zero percent chance of storm activity.[1] Today was the day we would be getting the ten hours of crucial car-in-motion photography. We mounted our process trailer with our oh-so-secret automobile prototype and began to head down the ten-mile stretch of city road the Mayor's Office had shut down for us.

Suddenly, someone radioed in a comment.

---

1 Tulsa, Oklahoma, stands slightly northeast of the center of a state known for its vast plains. These plains create an on-ramp for radical winds, much like a drag strip creates momentum for a powerful engine. This is where opposing weather fronts converge and violent storms result. Due to this unique attribute, winds blow new, unannounced weather in at radical speeds, rendering all weather predictions null and void. It is, in fact, quite challenging to come up with an occupation that is allowed more error than an Oklahoma weatherman—that tolerates inaccuracy. To this end, the forecast may state a zero percent chance of storm activity—but if, in fact, the tornadoes come, the weatherman is forgiven as long as, on the next show, he simply says "oops."

COMMENT: *I don't know if we should give this much attention, but the storm radar says something big is coming.*

MARK: How could that be? There isn't a cloud in the sky.

COMMENT: *I'm just telling you the truth.*

MARK: I'm directing a film. I don't want you to tell me the truth. I want you to tell me what I want to hear.

COMMENT: *What should we do?*

MARK: You know how wrong these weather guys are. If it's real, it's hours away. We've got plenty of time. Let's roll.

So, roll we indeed did. We pulled out of the parking lot near downtown Tulsa with pristine blue sky above us. We drove through the gorgeous decades-old trees down Riverside Drive, ignorant of the fact that before we drove back up this road, half of them would be felled across power lines and throughways. We drove past the view of the glass-exteriored Williams Building downtown—not realizing that the next time we looked its direction, the windows would be blown out, and my mother-in-law would be trapped in its stairwell.

A dozen of us traveled, strapped in (though standing) on a large wooden trailer taking up two full lanes of traffic. The prototype vehicle sat secured onto it, exposed to the elements. Three actors inside. Hundreds of thousands of dollars of equipment outside. And then suddenly, our Los Angeles client saw something in the distance.

CLIENT: *Why is it daytime over here and nighttime over there?*

MARK: Where over there?

CLIENT: *Over there where the lightning is having a party and the black mass of clouds are funneling down toward land.*

MARK: Oh. That would be the storm they mentioned.

CLIENT:	*You said we had plenty of time.*
MARK:	Well. Isn't that a funny thing.
CLIENT:	*It looks bad. Will we die?*
MARK:	Sure.

We raced down Riverside Drive toward the other end of town: a trek that should have taken at least forty-five minutes traveling the speed one should not exceed with an apparatus of this complexity. We were going as fast as we thought possible—until the temperature dropped twenty-five degrees.

CLIENT:	*Say. It just got really cold.*
MARK:	Mmhm.
CLIENT:	*What is that the crew guys are screaming?*
MARK:	Those are strong and multiple profanities.
CLIENT:	*I see. Does that mean the temperature changing is a bad thing?*
MARK:	Yes. I believe it does mean that. Yes.
CLIENT:	*What sort of bad thing?*
MARK:	Well, a drastic change in temperature normally signifies two things.
CLIENT:	*Number one?*
MARK:	That we are about to be pummeled with hail, more than likely destroying the car.
CLIENT:	*And yet you are strangely at peace.*
MARK:	That's because of number two.
CLIENT:	*Which is?*
MARK:	We are directly underneath a tornado that could, at any moment, hurl us to our deaths, so why worry about the automobile?
CLIENT:	*Oh. So—maybe we should pray then.*
MARK:	And then perhaps a string of strong and multiple profanities.

At that exact moment, no one was hesitant to pray.

The driver of the trailer, Kent, hurried us to the first sign of shelter. Unfortunately, the first sign of shelter was underneath a highway overpass which, in a tornado, is the safety equivalent of laying a kitten on a stove eye. After much argument, we were moved underneath the awning of an abandoned gas station just as the gusts of wind were causing treetops to flex horizontally. We rushed into a nearby ice cream establishment and began to truly process what this meant for our schedule, not to mention impending damage.

CLIENT: *This is bad. This is really bad.*

MARK: Oh, this is just Tulsa. We get storms like this all the time.

KEVIN: Incorrect answer, Mark.

MARK: What I mean to say is that this is the storm of the century, unlike any other storm in our state's history. It is a Noahic reckoning of historic proportions.

KEVIN: That is also an incorrect answer.

CLIENT: *This is just bad. I mean, the Japanese gentlemen were really starting to like you, and they were talking about potentially doing another project with your team in Tulsa—*

MARK: They were?

CLIENT: *But this—I mean, we have earthquakes, but this—*

MARK: They were talking about potentially—

CLIENT: *I hope this doesn't sour them on Oklahoma.*

KEVIN: Me too.

MARK: Where are they? I don't see them.

KEVIN: They didn't come with us this time.

MARK: They didn't?! Where are they?!

CLIENT: *They're back at the base, huddled with eight other people in the bathtub.*

This was, of course, true. And why wouldn't it be? Why wouldn't the most esteemed gentlemen we had ever worked with end up packed with a half-dozen college interns in a stranger's bathtub?

So, now, the worrying truly began. It turns out that as we were speeding down Riverside Drive, the radio news was reporting our predicament to the rest of the city. Meanwhile, the window next to my mother-in-law's desk at work imploded, sending her screaming into the stairwell. Simultaneously, the Bartlett pear tree in my own front yard snapped like a toothpick and collapsed. This convergence of three panics caused my daughter Morgan to break into the utmost level of hysteria. The result: I am standing in the vestibule of the ice cream shop, watching as entire trees fly past the window, screaming to be heard over the wind to my young daughter on the cell phone in order to calm her down because it seems as if the book of Revelation has come to fruition. At the same time, our crew is working to relax the talent while a conference cell phone call begins with California to assess damage, and our two respected international guests hunker down fifteen miles away while trying not to slip on the Irish Spring.

It was a banner day for all.

Two hours later, it was over. The sun shone again. The weather declared that no tornado had, in fact, occurred—only radical blasts of wind ranging from eighty to one hundred miles an hour that held the power and damage of a tornado. The difference: the wind did not "swirl"—this was somehow expected to be comforting. We made the national news. The local affiliate dubbed it a "gustado," a term that was more than likely inaccurate—not that this would matter in their highly accountable line of work.

The vehicle was not harmed.

The actors were calmed.

The crew reduced the immediate use of profanity.

And our guests of honor squeezed out of the bathtub.

The drive back up Riverside Drive toward our home base was filled with anxiety. Our Japanese friends had been considering future work with us without our knowledge, and before we could celebrate that fact, it seemed like a lost cause. Why would anyone want to return to our beautiful town after realizing that once a summer it felt like Judgment Day?

We made the most of the remainder of the afternoon and evening, capturing another entire sequence. The next few days, we were aggressive to make up lost time. At the end of the week, we had all the footage we needed in the can, and it was time for the vehicle, and our Japanese friends, to head home.

We asked the group out to dinner to celebrate a successful production. It was here that we hoped to thank them and somehow resurrect consideration for future work. We would finally have the conversation. The revelation of their assessment of what it was like to bring a one-of-a-kind vehicle all that way just to have it threatened by hail damage and the queen mother of storms. This was the conversation we expected.

But it was not the conversation we received.

Of the many praising and congratulatory comments our friends made at that dinner table, the most humbling and startling was the primary reason why they said those things—yes, they did indeed intend to bring us more work and find more ways to have their productions travel to Tulsa. The reason?

There was something different about the people.

The interpreter informed us of the deep level of enjoyment they were celebrating. Of the working relationships—the friendships they felt had been established. Of the common artistic language we held that superseded our barriers of dialect. Of the fact that they felt we had truly been ourselves and that—though they were not able to put their finger on it—there was something truly different about us. Something very joyful. Something that celebrated life. Something at peace. That something was revealed through our smiles and our behavior, through our work ethic and problem-solving when storms collided. Through our respect to them as foreign guests. Through our sheer enjoyment of our craft and one another. Mutual respect for all involved. A true team effort. They expressed how different this experience was from their other experiences in production on either coast and in other countries.

For these reasons, they expressed a sincere desire to work with us again very soon. To work with us—yes, for the sake of another great project—but also for a more important purpose.

To discover what it was that was truly different.

And where we had been hesitant to give the clues of that which truly differentiates us, it had never dawned on us that these men had been watching. Marinating in the experience for a week like a good steak ready to be bitten. Unfazed by the storm, but rather observing. Observing to see if the storm would break us or if the difference in us was stronger than a gustado.

The only reason I passed this test was because I did not realize I was being tested. I was simply enjoying what I was built to do while someone else watched. Celebrating the Creator's gifts with great joy and responsibility instead of looking over my shoulder and trying to pretend or play the part of the example. It worked because there was no desperate attempt. We legitimately grew to care for them and they for us. And without expecting it to happen, they witnessed something deeper than we realized we were revealing.

A true impression.

Believe me, I had made great and epic attempts to leave impressions on others before. But my own vain attempts always led to the same mistake: the impression that remained was my own face.

But, this time, the attempt was not on purpose. The sentiment was not "Watch me watch God!" And, because of this, the face left behind was Someone else's completely. They ignored me and saw through the surface to Him who holds my true joy in the palm of His hand.

They had softened. We had bitten. And the teethmarks remained.

And all because—through some miracle of moments—we ended up in the center of the same storm and came out the other side changed.

love bites
—FEATURING—
"THE WIT AND WISDOM OF DEF LEPPARD"

Def Leppard. Weren't they a heavy metal band from the eighties?

Correction: a hair metal band.

What's the difference?

Heavy metal bands worship Satan. Hair metal bands worship their hair.

Ah. And I remember that song.

Those are actually the only two words I remember from that song.

They're the only two words you can comprehend in that song.

No. I think there's a statement about "zimmy liddo high, zimmy liddo low, zimmy liddo heddo, let's go!" somewhere in there. I understood that.

You're thinking of "Pour Some Sugar on Me."

And, of course, the Scriptures would concur.

With Def Leppard?

Well—just those two words.

That love bites?

It does indeed. Love bites. Love bleeds.

See—and in college, I was under the impression that was a bad thing.

Well, I'm probably not using it in the same
context as the Leppard intended.

Did they have the one-armed drummer?

Deep down, aren't we all one-armed drummers?

Get to the point.

The point is that real and actual love does not often look like
what we think it does.

That it bites?

That we would prefer our love to be selfish, pleasing ourselves most of all.
We expect love to kiss. But true love is aggressive and attentive and changes
things, wakes us from our stupor of danger—motivates, stings,
rebukes—while still gently caressing.

And that's a bite?

A truer statement would be that love knows. That it is aware.
That it remembers and demands our remembrance right back.
This is how God loves us, and it is how we are expected to love others.
It is the only love that will leave teethmarks.
All other love leaves a flashbang.

There's a problem I have, though, with the whole teethmarks idea.

Fair enough.

*You're insinuating that we have control over what sort of marks
are left when we are only the teeth. The person we are trying to
affect is the skin. We don't have any control over whether or not
that skin is rough or tender.*

I never said to bite the moment you begin to love.
Yes, true love is aggressive, but—like I just said—it is also
attentive. It is aware of when one is ready to be bitten.
When the bite will leave something behind.

Marinating.

Yes. When God loves us, He saturates us with Himself in order that our
discovery of Him be real and legitimate. We each begin to discover how
much beauty is around us, and we begin to notice His touch and His plan.
Once we embrace Him and say, "I am soft now—I don't only want
you to be *the* God, I want you to be *my* God"—that is when He gets
aggressive and changes us. The unexpected twist is that He changes us
by allowing us to change others. We follow His example. We
get into others' lives. We are attentive. We help meet their needs and
reveal to them God's beauty. This softens them until the point when
they are prepared to have a true scar of love left behind.

Isn't that manipulation?

It is if you don't truly believe God and love the people.
If you try to soften people to change them to your whims so you have
another notch on your belt, you will fail anyway.
But it is not manipulation at all to love someone so much
that you respond to their needs in a way that reveals
your God is real and true and will change them.
It is not human to love others unconditionally. It can only be spiritual.

Let's go back to an idea you mentioned briefly.

The worshipping of hair?

No. After that. You said love remembers.

Well, isn't that what a scar is?

A remembrance?

Something indelible that causes us to learn.
Ignorance forgets. But love remembers.

Like the way married couples hold grudges.

No.

Maybe you should explain a little more.

Recently I did the "read the Bible through in a year" plan.

Impressive. How long did it take you?

Two years, eight months.

Forget what I said about impressive.

I was looking for the common theme that connected
all the books together because I've always been a little nonplussed
by the genealogy chapters where they list
367 unpronounceable names in one sitting.

You don't enjoy those?

Not a big fan. No.

So, did you come up with anything?

In fact—I did.

And?

Every book of the Bible does have one central theme
in common, and it was a vastly important lesson for me.

The tension is mounting.

Never forget God.

Okay. Now, I'm intrigued.

Well—think about it. Why would those genealogies be there in the first
place? It means that history is extremely important to God. How we got
to where we are—how we learned what we learned—and how God made
it all happen. God gets the people in the Bible out of scrape after scrape
and tragedy after tragedy because—let's face it—a lot of those guys made
some really bad choices. But the grandest mistake of all is that after God
would help them, rescue them, or change them, they would have a tendency
to eventually forget. So God appears as fire and smoke to remind them.
He has them build a tabernacle. He sends tablets of stone down from the
mountain. He puts a ram in a bush and a star in the east and a rainbow in
the sky and a child in an animal trough and sends prophets and psalmists
and judges and angels and dreams and goes to the great lengths necessary
so that we are constantly reminded that He loves us and does not want us
to FORGET that He loves us because when we forget
that He loves us—bad things happen.

Why do bad things happen?

Because when we forget that He is God,
we have a tendency to believe that we are.

Oh.

We might not say it or think we believe it,
but our actions speak otherwise.
It is in these forgetful moments where
we become petty and self-involved—
proprietary and indignant.
This is when our acts of so-called love are truly for our own benefit.
And these acts leave no true indentation.
Because the truth of the matter is
we have no right or reason to forget God.

Don't you think that's a little unfair?

In what way?

*In many ways. Many aren't softened enough yet
to catch on to the fact that God is there.
Are you saying that they have no right to forget God?*

Yes.

Why?

Because God has never forgotten them.
Many think God has forgotten them,
and this is why they do not believe.
But He has never stopped reaching for their hand
regardless of how withdrawn it may be from Him.
We make decisions—or others do—
that place our own lives in a compromising position.

And we are so quick to claim that God's hand has been withdrawn.
But the truth is no matter how much damage we do to God's reputation,
He is continually reaching out in new attentive ways.
If the sunrise doesn't work, He'll go for a miracle.
If that doesn't work—the still small moment.
Whatever it takes—He keeps reaching until His hand is slapped aside.
And even in that case, He will reach again.
Because He never forgets us.

But even though this is how we were each eventually reached,
we have an inclination to forget what sort of love was actually effective
and refuse that love to others around us.
So we give our own version of what we label love—the counterfeit.
And we push and we pull and we bite, and we are suddenly so surprised
when there is no evidence that our love was ever there.

But God is concerned for His Holy Name,
which has been dishonored by His people throughout the world.
Dishonored by us.
Dishonored by counterfeit love.

And it's time to change course.
To remember Him. To honor Him with our actions.

And for those actions to indeed leave teethmarks.

dumb SHOW

Am I supposed to automatically know what a dumbshow is?

It's not a thing. It's a stage term. And it doesn't have an article before it.

An article?

It's not "a" dumbshow. It's just dumbshow.

You made this up.

No. But I do appreciate the vote of confidence.

If it airs on the Fox Network, is it automatically a dumbshow?

You're digressing again.

Or if it has people in bee costumes.

It's not a program. It's an act. It's something you do.

I do?

Something an actor does on stage.

And this is actually going to apply here?

Oh—you just wait.

Because clearly you aren't going to explain before another story.

A very important story.

Is it a story that uses whimsy to teach the human reproduction system?

No. You're thinking of an "after school" story.

Then, what makes your story so important?

The president of the United States.

Is it too late to learn about reproduction?

applause for a stagedive
—OR—
JUST AS I BEGAN THE CARTWHEEL

The Brothers Grimm did not, in fact, write a fairy tale titled "The President and the Parasite," but, if they had, I would have been the central tragic figure.

Not that I should complain. Any story including the president is destined to be a strong anecdote, especially if the teller is a character in the story. This has actually been proven. For instance, consider the following conversation:

> MARK:　　　I had macaroni and cheese for dinner.
> YOU:　　　*That's not interesting.*
> MARK:　　　With the president of the United States.
> YOU:　　　*Really? Tell me all about it.*

Or even this conversation:

> MARK:　　　I pushed a two-year-old off a swing at the park.
> YOU:　　　*That's horrible!*
> MARK:　　　With the president of the United States.
> YOU:　　　*Awesome!*

Regardless of the tale that is told, being a character in a story with the president may make one seem important or perhaps influential. Though, I promise, this story will make me seem neither.

As I have mentioned enough times for it to be considered desperate, I am a comic. Due to the fact that money exchanges hands for no other reason than being ridiculous, there are certain benchmarks a comic looks for to validate his existence. These benchmarks include, but are not limited to, the following:

1. Hosting gala events.
2. Serious dramatic roles.
3. Leno or Letterman.
4. Writing a memoir that repeatedly reminds the reader that the writer is a comic.
5. Receiving gift baskets from Harry & David.
6. A sitcom.
7. Performing for important people.

When your trade is making people happy for only one hour of their life, you take what peripheral healthy gratification you can get. This is why, in January of 2001, I was surprised to receive that random phone call.

It must first be understood that I was not on the hunt for a challenging opportunity at the moment. My career was going well, and my family and I had a surplus of finances as well as lots of leftover nonperishable goods from the predicted doomsday a year earlier when all the world had been expected to implode into tiny flecks of matter because a computer could not count past midnight. The question of the millennium was supposed to be "How now shall we survive?" It, in fact, became "What are we going to do with all this canned meat?"

So, I sat at my desk—merrily finishing up another can of ham—when the phone rang.

I do not declare to be prophetic, but when a phone rings, I always have a sense of what the ring means. I know when it is my wife startled by a hamster. I know when it is a disgruntled client. I know when it is a solicitor. I know when it is finally the response to a call I made three weeks prior. I know when it is Bono (though it has never been, but I am certain I will know). And I know when it is an immense opportunity.

I must have known. Because, for some reason, I had the wherewithal to remove the portions of pre-chewed meatlike product from my mouth and spit them into the napkin that others might call a W-2 form. At the very last moment, I picked up the phone and answered with my genius voice:

MARK: THIS IS MARK STEELE.

As if the caller had woven his or her way through eleven cryptic phone puzzles to discover the prize at the end, which was I. The reason this was pivotal to the story was because there were three other ways I could have answered the phone:

1. Pretending I had just been awakened.
2. Asking if I could take their food order.
3. Speaking Ewok.

Due to an abnormal moment of professionalism, I answered assertively and discovered that the individual on the other end was booking entertainment for the inauguration of President George W. Bush and wanted to see if I was interested in performing: an opportunity I absolutely knew I was going to accept—not realizing, of course, that it would be the most unique comedy experience of my lifetime.

There are several close competitors in the running for the second most unique comedy experience of my lifetime. Performing for eight people at a house of pancakes, performing for eight thousand people who all thought they had bought tickets to see someone else, and performing an improv comic mystery musical that resulted in stunned silence from the audience—these all rank highly on the list. But they do not come in second.

Second place is reserved for a performance marred by mass confusion.

The opportunity began innocuously enough. I was in college, and the comedy troupe I was spearheading at the time was granted an offer to perform sketch comedy and improv to a group of missionaries in Oklahoma. These were individuals who, we were told, had been hard at work on the field for a lengthy period of time and needed a vacation. They needed a laugh. It sounded remarkably like the type of job our team embraced because the audience deserved to laugh and would be tired (therefore laughing easily). We agreed to the job and began scripting and rehearsing a few weeks out.

I spoke with the contact for the dinner a few times in the following weeks: confirming load-in and set-up times, show length, the fee—those sorts of things.

When the day of performance arrived, I showed up at the hall a few hours before we were to go on in order to set up some of our gear. The contact and I enjoyed a little bit of small talk.

Then, as I was about to walk out the door, he dropped the most peculiar question.

"Do you mind if I ask you something?"

"No problem."

"Just out of curiosity, while doing sketch comedy, how do you get past that hurdle?"

The knots in my stomach began to tighten the way they do when I know a solicitor is on the other end of the ringing phone.

"What hurdle is that?"

"You know—the language barrier."

ME: Are you serious?

HER: *Of course I'm serious. You are Mark Steele?*

ME: Yes. I am Mark Steele. That's why I answered the phone by saying, "This is Mark Steele."

HER: *You've come highly recommended.*

ME: You're kidding.

HER: *No. We were looking for someone different than the usual.*

ME: You mean someone unknown.

HER: *Well—someone who is actually funny.*

ME: Yeah. I would imagine you don't find too many entertaining conservatives.

(Complete silence.)

                In the arts, I mean.

HER: *I didn't realize comedy was an art.*

ME: Can we pretend I haven't started talking yet?

HER: *You're fine. And, of course, you will need to audition.*

ME: Of course. Really?

HER: *Of course.*

ME:	Yes. Of course. And how might I do that?
HER:	*Well, have you done any political comedy lately?*
ME:	None that I would want you to hear.
HER:	*You might want to pull back on the honesty a bit.*
ME:	Sure. It's a bad habit.
HER:	*Could you put some jokes on paper?*
ME:	Sure. If I can find some paper that doesn't have canned meat on it. Does the president want any canned meat?
HER:	*He has plenty.*
ME:	Yes. I could certainly put some political humor on paper.
HER:	*But nothing too harsh. Unless it's aimed at liberals. God wants us to love everyone. Except liberals.*
ME:	In comedy, we don't call it hate. We call it "satire."
HER:	*Why?*
ME:	There's nothing in the Bible about satire.
HER:	*Ah. And you don't mind writing some of this satire?*
ME:	I can feel the venom dripping already.
HER:	*In politics, we call that venom "righteous indignation."*
ME:	Can I use that?
HER:	*No.*

So the audition on paper began. I crafted many audacious and biting plays on words. The sort of things that would have gotten me expelled from high school, but were somehow acceptable aimed at those who benefit from my taxes. I submitted a sample of my current act along with the jokes and waited.

Weeks went by.

As time passed and I realized that the inauguration was one week away, I assumed my involvement had been declined. I was just about to walk on stage in Seattle when the phone rang.

ME:	Erheek Abloo?
HER:	*Excuse me?*
ME:	Sorry. I was speaking Ewok.
HER:	*Well, Mr. Steele, we reviewed your tape and your content, and we would love to have you be a part of our celebration and perform for the president.*
ME:	Really?!
HER:	*You still kinda need to work on that poker face.*
ME:	No. I mean—I wasn't expecting this because it's taken so long.
HER:	*Oh. We made our decision weeks ago, but, of course, we couldn't let you know that until it was closer to the time.*
ME:	Why not?
HER:	*Because of security.*
ME:	You have security concerns about me?
HER:	*Not at all.*
ME:	I don't understand.
HER:	*It's just protocol.*
ME:	To have concerns about security when there are no concerns about security?
HER:	*Precisely.*
ME:	I understand.

I was elated. So much for these peons in Seattle. I was going to the real Washington. The smaller one. I waltzed out onto stage with all the confidence in the world and nailed the performance. It was a banner day.

After my set, I did my best to both walk in humility and bask in name-dropping.

> *I love it here in Washington, D.C. Did I say D.C.?*
> *I meant Seattle. D.C. is where I'm going next weekend.*
> *Ask me why.*

> *This is a great sandwich. Almost as great as the sandwich*
> *I will be eating Friday evening backstage as I wait to*
> *meet the president!*
> *Ask me what kind of sandwich.*

> *That poor woman just tripped over her shoelace.*
> *I hope I don't trip over my shoelace on Friday*
> *when I perform for the president!*
> *Ask me if I think you're proud of me.*

My brother, Dav, decided we should celebrate with some pizza in the hotel room. We did, though I refused to drink soda as I didn't want to be bloated from sodium when meeting W. For some reason, this hotel had no bottled water machines, so I did something I had not done in years.

I drank water from the tap.

There are many bad decisions that are foreseeable. Many ruinous choices that we kick ourselves for later due to the fact that the neon sign was flashing "WARNING" very clearly. But there are some bad decisions that can only be seen through hindsight, probably because they are the choices that end up biting you on the hind. Some decisions that seemed like the most innocent choices at the time. These decisions are the ones that tend to mark our life for posterity. And drinking water from the Seattle hotel faucet was precisely this type of decision.

"The what barrier?"

"You know—how on earth do you perform comedy where the lines are important when no one can understand you?"

"Why on earth would I ever perform for people who can't understand me?"

The contact literally grabbed his face, "Did I forget to tell you?"

"Tell me what?"

"Oh. I did it again. I'm so sorry."

"You did what again?

"I forgot something important. You see, your audience tonight are all Mandarin Chinese. Not one of them speaks a lick of English."

Yes. He had, in fact, forgotten to fill me in on this fact earlier. Now, there we were with barely an hour to spare before performing two hours' worth of English-only comedy to 250 Chinamen.

"I wouldn't worry about it though."

"Why not?"

"If you can't get them to laugh, just start waving your arms a lot. They love that."

I really did. I thought it was only nerves. I mean, yes, the flu had been going around, and I had been working hard—but the fact remained that I believed I was having chronic stomach pains because of the performance of a lifetime that was to be held within the next twenty-four hours.

I had not been this ill since the gall bladder removal, and I was, of course, worried that the sickness would keep me off that airplane. But Friday approached, and I hunkered down and picked myself up out of bed to get my hind to D.C.

As the plane was landing, I felt my stomach lurch for the twenty-seventh time that week. Only this time, it brought with it a case of the cold sweats. My palms were sweating. My scalp. The small skinfolds behind my knees. I felt both cold/clammy and scorching/scalding simultaneously. The type of sickness that is marked by a shift from self-pity to self-concern. I set down my pen right smack in the middle of the construction of a Daniel Patrick Moynihan joke (God rest his soul) and braced myself on the retractable tray table that was not allowed to be down because it clearly had the ability to flay me in half if the plane swerved.

I closed my eyes and had a conversation with myself.

Not now. Anything but now.

You can't control it. You can't determine with your will whether or not you are going to get sick.

I'm not going to get sick. I AM sick.
I'm trying to stop from getting even sicker.

Note to self: anxiety concerning a job while getting on a plane does not equal a healthier stomach.

I only have to make it through today.

If I can just get through the next ten hours,
I can get sick all I want tomorrow.

What are you worried about? Pain has always benefited you.

What are you talking about?

*In comedy. You tell your stories about your gall bladder and
you do your physical comedy where you fall and beat yourself
up, and they laugh. What's that called?*

Dumbshow.

*Yeah. You do the whole dumbshow bit where you fall down on purpose.
The stagedive. That always gets a laugh.*

When do I do that?

In that one bit. That Whitney Houston thing you do.

That's not falling down. That's dancing.

Right. Same thing. You throw yourself on the ground and stuff.

It's called a cartwheel.

Yeah. But it's very vulnerable.

True. And it hurts.

You see. Hurt works for you on stage. That's why you let them see your pain.

I don't let them see the real pain. Just the lighter version.
The funny version that doesn't complicate things.

Yeah. Dumbshow. It's like you make the pain unpainful.
They love that. So, see. You've got nothing to be afraid of.

But what I'm feeling right now is actual pain. Not a cover.

It's not a cover when you do it on stage either. It's real.
You tell the true stories. You really feel the fall.

But it's not real.

Why not.

Because I don't let the audience know that the pain matters.

Bummer.

And this pain right now definitely matters.
I don't know if I'm going to be able to go on.

Sure you will. You always go on.
You went on for the half-dozen people at the pancake breakfast.

Yes.

You went on when the eight thousand people booed you because the
headliner didn't tell them he wasn't coming.

True. But I didn't let them see the real pain.

What about the missionaries?

Excuse me?

The Mandarin Chinese missionaries. Almost ten years ago.

Do you remember them?

How could I forget them?

You should never forget them.

And why is that?

Because that pain was not staged.

I was speechless. We had opened with our sure-fire bit. Our musical number. And they just stared—250 Asians, mouths actually slightly dropped.

Now don't get me wrong. They were smiling. Very wide, in fact. They seemed to be enjoying the moment—or perhaps "enjoyment" isn't as accurate as, say, "bewilderment."

The problem in our minds was that, though we felt we had better comedy bits coming, they were all dialogue-driven. We had just performed our choreographed number. If that one didn't make them laugh, we had very little hope that anything else coming would. It was now time for the monologue—often the most disastrous portion of our show.

I stood on stage with my comedy partner, Tony, and watched in awe as he stepped up to the edge of the stage and went further off-script than I had expected. I could never recall the actual statement, but it went something along these lines:

TONY: To tell you the truth, none of us speak your
                  language. We didn't know until a little while ago
                  that you didn't understand English. It's very
                  important to us that you have a good time, but
                  we're feeling a bit awkward—so what do you say
                  we just give it our best shot and all enjoy this
                  night together regardless?

*To this day, I don't have the foggiest idea what that
crowd of people thought Tony said, but I have a theory.*

*I believe they heard his spirit and that it transcended
language. He spoke with truth and hope and with a love
he had for them—and they understood him.*

*They began to applaud. And cheer. And smile. They
wanted more. Much more. Ninety minutes more.*

*It remains to this day one of the most joyous
performances of my career. We, as a troupe, moved
with great abandon, with a recklessness of comedy.
We aimed to make ourselves laugh and, in the process,
brought the house down.*

*Would I like to repeat this experience with another
English-free crowd? Not on your life. But it continues,
to this day, to reveal to me the power of letting those
watching see my real pain—to see the scars of my
remembrance—and to hope that the staring begins to
heal the pain inside of themselves.*

*And that, Mr. Contact, is how we deal with the language
barrier.*

Of course I remember them.

So, don't be afraid.

I can't help it. I can't remember ever feeling this horrible.

I have a feeling all of this is going to turn around into
a story that you will tell for years and years.

Sure. But what kind of story?

Relax. It's a story that includes the president.
How bad could it get?

My cab pulled up to the swank hotel in the heart of D.C. where the
inauguration ball would be held. I stood on the corner of the busy
intersection, soaking the moment in. I headed downstairs to the ballroom,
assuming I would find a group setting up for the evening. Instead, I
discovered, to my surprise, an entirely separate gathering of media pundits
from national news networks, all gathered for the inauguration. They were
having some sort of fruit and pastry breakfast, which I would imagine
was labeled "continental" and considered insufficient. Not that I would
necessarily picture a network news scrambled egg buffet, though that might
please the weathermen. As they discussed journalistic integrity or some
other oxymoron, the woman who had hired me for the event suddenly
appeared behind me. She informed me that the media conference was
going slightly overtime and that we would be setting up shortly.

ME:	Hopefully the news people will all be gone
	before the president gets here.
HER:	(laughing) *Wow. You really are funny.*
ME:	Thank you.

HER:		*As if the president will actually be here.*
ME:		The president isn't going to be here?
HER:		*Of course not. You're hilarious.*
ME:		But, isn't this his inaugural ball?
HER:		Yes, *but the president has six or seven*
		inaugural balls.
ME:		How many does he go to?
HER:		*Maybe two.*
ME:		What are the chances this is one of those two?
HER:		*Slim to none. He declined our invitation.*
ME:		You said we would be performing for
		the president.
HER:		*Yes. "For."*
ME:		But not actually "in front of."
HER:		*Heavens, no.*
ME:		Then why could you not tell me until the last
		minute that I was chosen due to security?
HER:		*Because there will be many other prominent*
		Washingtonians here tonight.
ME:		Oh. Okay.
HER:		*Dignitaries and representatives from the House*
		and perhaps a senator or two.
ME:		Well—that's a good thing, then.
HER:		*Oh, yes. A very good thing. And many television*
		evangelists.
ME:		Many what?
HER:		*Television evangelists.*
ME:		I have a really good guess as to why the president
		declined that invitation.
HER:		*I'm still hanging on to that slim-to-none chance.*
ME:		And I don't think Washingtonians is a real word.

The evening wore on, and I awaited my turn backstage as dignitary upon dignitary did, in fact, arrive. I was scheduled to go on at 8:15 p.m. But each half-hour continued to drag onward: eight-thirty, nine, nine-thirty. I was feeling so ill that I thought I might explode, but I was afraid to go to the bathroom to throw up in case that precise moment came when I would be called on stage.

Ten—ten-thirty—

I couldn't take it anymore. I didn't know it was possible to have both a high fever and cold sweats, but I had them, and they were tremendous. The churning in my body continued.

Eleven.

I began to recall my gall bladder experience. My bad omelette. Every instance where this inner twisting had occurred. My suspicions were confirmed: this time was worse than all of the others combined. I placed my head in my hands and breathed deeply. Certainly, it would be any moment now. I mean, I was only performing for fifteen minutes. How much longer could it take? I couldn't wait any longer. I would go to the bathroom right now and take my chances.

The stage manager briskly stuck his head into my dressing room. "Five minutes, Mr. Steele."

Five minutes? I can't get to the bathroom and back in five minutes! What is five plus fifteen? That's twenty. Twenty more minutes. I can do that. Will power. I can breathe deeply. I can make it through twenty more minutes. Come on, Steele. Suck it up.

It's for the president.

I took my place on stage amid much hesitant applause. Politicians are never certain whether or not to embrace comedians until they have heard what side they are taking. I began my rants. I volleyed the jokes into a successful rhythm. Bang. Bang. Bang. I was on. The Washingtonians were with me. A zinger here, an ad lib there. I was feeling good. My flop sweat disappeared. I was in the zone. I knew I had the closer, the golden one-liner to wrap up the set. I let it loose and waved "thank you, goodnight" amid a flurry of applause. I had succeeded, and I had not had to show them my pain.

But, as I exited the stage, a curious thing happened.

The stage manager grabbed me by the arm as I was walking away.

"They want more."

More? What more could they want?

And that is when the woman who hired me approached.

HER:	*Great set! They are loving you!*
ME:	Thank you.
HER:	*You have to do more.*
ME:	I didn't prepare any more.
HER:	*You have to do Whitney.*

Which is when the pain suddenly came back.

ME:	Whitney? What do you mean?
HER:	*The Whitney Houston dance! You must do the Whitney Houston dance!*
ME:	HOW DO YOU KNOW ABOUT THE WHITNEY HOUSTON DANCE?!
HER:	*We have a mutual friend.*
ME:	Let's consider "friend" a very loose term.
HER:	*You simply have to do it. They want more.*
ME:	So, that's it, then. I simply have to do it? I have to do somersaults and cartwheels with a high fever just because they want more?
HER:	*Mark?*
ME:	Don't say it.
HER:	*Do it for the president.*

Do it for our country. Push yourself into an aerobics-induced coma for this great nation. It will be worth it. The applause. The bragging rights. Just think of it—an encore at the inauguration. What would my children think? What would the world now finally comprehend concerning the healing power of comedy to unite the nations? I would be a legend. An icon. Remembered in my small town and larger circles for doing something great.

And it wouldn't really hurt all that much.

So, I gave the thumbs up. I walked back out onto the stage amid great applause. The lights went down. The music began.

I gave the performance of a lifetime.

And, just as I began the cartwheel—I crapped in my own trousers.

tumbling off the highwire
—AND—
"LIVING TO TELL ABOUT IT"

I literally loaded my pants in front of senators and representatives. I emptied my colon for Colin. I did a number two for the number one. I soiled myself for the president.

It turns out that I didn't have the flu after all. For some reason, that one glass of tap water in Seattle had given me a little friend. The aforementioned parasite. And, as much as I did not want to reveal my inner pain to that elite and dignified group, the terror inside of me decided to rear its ugly head at the single most unfortunate moment of my career.

After all the tripping and flailing, the cartwheels and somersaults, the bruises and stagedives that I had submitted myself to for the sake of a laugh and an ovation, this one time the pain had not been staged. I was not falling down on purpose just to gain sympathy. I was wide open.

It is not until you live a moment wide open that you truly discover the difference between actual sacrifice and artificial endeavors that point the finger at your own supposed profundity.

Sure, I believe I am being vulnerable when I select a few inconsistencies, issues, or hurts in my own life for others to take a good look at, and then I wonder why no one takes interest.

It is because the revelation of the pain in question is so well-orchestrated and so rehearsed that it smells like manipulation. But I tend to believe that because I have uncovered any humanness at all in myself that I should be applauded as a saint and martyr.

That, indeed, is the dumbshow: the intentional tripping up or falling down, the revealing of a flaw for the sake of applause and attention. This is not vulnerability. This is not abandon. This is not sacrifice. But it is too often mistaken for all of these.

*flash*BANG

It is actual truth that changes others. Actual truth coming out of ourselves. Not orchestrated truth. Not partial truth that is well-timed. Not "just enough to matter"—but rather the whole enchilada.

Does this mean every other person needs to see every wart and blemish inside of me? No, it does not. But it does mean that if I truly desire to be God's instrument of change to others, I have to be willing and unguarded. I have to be open to the fact that He may ask that I reveal some of my flaws and hurts to those I least want to when I least want to do it.

That is the difference between a grenade and a flashbang. A flashbang only lets out what is impressive while a grenade throws every bit of itself out there when the pin is pulled.

That doesn't sound right.

What?

Every bit of myself?
It doesn't sound healthy to be an open book to everyone.

I didn't say that.

Then, what are you saying? Because I've done this, you know.
I've been unguarded with people I thought were godly—
people I thought I could trust. And when they ended up not being trustworthy,
I hated—literally hated—that I had given them any information whatsoever.
I don't think it is safe to throw every bit of myself out there.

I didn't say it was safe. I said it will change people.

At my expense.

Yes.
Look, I do think there is a significant difference
between being vulnerable and being foolhardy.

You do have to be careful who you let into
your inner circle of accountability. That is not what I'm saying.

It sounds like it is exactly what you are saying.

To play your problems on a loudspeaker for
all to hear would be foolish and ineffective.

But probably entertaining.

To everyone but yourself, perhaps.
But this is about the fact that many who believe they are just being
guarded are actually imprisoning themselves.
This is not about stating everything to everyone.
This is about being open to God saying
"this truth to this person right now."
To be completely guarded, where that is not an option,
is to live in fear of the truth.
A healthy individual keeps the darkest parts of the truth
in the open for the circle he or she can trust to be around.
But that person is no longer afraid of that truth
because it is in the light to someone else.
That is when that truth loses its chains and instead holds power.
The power to heal others.
We believe we are healing others when we reveal a truth of our choosing.
A truth that isn't that big a deal to us—
that we have grown comfortable with.
We believe we are being quite impressive.
But all it communicates is that there are limits
on what the light should expose.
And that the darkness which holds others captive should remain secret.

But it should not.

I remember the first time I saw a tightrope walker at the circus.
I had seen them on television many times, but on television,
it was clear that there was a net.
At this live circus, I searched the floor of the big top with my eyes.
There was no net. Clearly no net!
Nothing to catch this individual if he were to fall.
I mentioned this to my mother,
and she assured me that the tightrope walker
had done this many times without falling.
But that was not good enough for me.
What if this was the one time he did indeed fall?
What if all that practice was suddenly for nothing
because no precautions had been taken?
I was desperately afraid to watch but couldn't keep my eyes away.
My heart was beating so fast.
And then it happened.

He made it to the other side?

No. He fell.

He what?!

He fell.

Did he die?

No.

But, I thought you said there was no net.

I was correct. There was no net.

Then how did he not die?

Because he never got close to the ground.
You see, I was so busy looking below him,
that it didn't dawn on me that
there might be something above him.

He was hooked to a wire.

He was indeed.
He was hooked in from above.
It was something I had never seen before.
So it didn't dawn on me to even look there.
But, somehow, in our own lives, we think it's going to be different.
We think, "Hey—I'll impress these people, show them
I am human. I'll tumble off the highwire
and fall into the net again and again and again."
But, truth is, that does nothing for people.
Because they see that there are nets.
They know the problems in their own lives that have nets,
so they are not surprised when there is a net waiting for you.
But, what about the other problems in their lives?

The problems that have no net.

The hurts and fears that have always seemed hopeless.
That have made them feel like a secret.
A freak.
A failure.
What about the problems that they are certain have no nets?
What if someone dared to reveal those
very same problems in their own life,
showing that the other person is not alone,
is not a freak,
and need not keep this secret?
That, unfortunately, we all have crapped our pants.

What would happen if that person tumbled off the highwire?
What would then be revealed?

That something is holding on from above.

And that is the truth that must be revealed.
That for every problem.
For every hurt and fear.
For every secret.
For every freak.
Something—
Someone is holding onto them from above.

That is the truth that changes people.

And I must stop being afraid to show it.

spit TAKE

Halfway through.

Yes. I am aware of that.

I'm only saying that because you've covered a lot of ground.

And?

And by now, I am certain you are running out of stories.

You only wish I was running out of stories.

Do people still say "you only wish"?

I'm nowhere near running out of stories.

I wish you were.

I know. That's why I said "you only wish."

What stories are left in your arsenal?

Hopefully, the sort that get the point across.

*What I mean to say is—what **manner** of stories are remaining?*

The stories that remain are either whimsical or shocking.

Oooh. Intriguing. How shocking?

Prepare yourself for the spittake.

losing face
WARNING:
THIS STORY CONTAINS
STEROIDS, AN INFECTION,
AND CHRISTIAN MUSIC

In the autumn of 1996, my wife Kaysie and I were in our eighteenth month of actively attempting to get pregnant. This is a thought that begins with exhilaration, but a process that begins with disappointment. Eighteen months later, the process was marred by a complete deflation of joy every thirty days. We began to question our ability and calling to have children.

Heartache after disappointment came and went eighteen times until the month of October. The thirty-first day, to be exact. I fell asleep the evening prior as my wife commented on how she felt "unusual." I was awakened at four in the morning to the only time in my life I have witnessed my wife weeping while staring at a stick on which she had recently urinated.

Our dream had come true. We were pregnant.

I used this phrase often, "We are pregnant." It was always interesting to say it to others. Easily, 99 percent of the listeners took offense at the choice of pronoun.

LISTENER:	*What do you mean by "we"?*
MARK:	We. Kaysie and I. We are both pregnant.
LISTENER:	*Oh—so you're both pregnant.*
MARK:	Well, we kinda both worked on it together. We thought we would, you know, celebrate together.

LISTENER:	*Let me get this straight. Kaysie has to carry a watermelon around for nine months, then pass it painfully while you read and nod, and you are both pregnant?*
MARK:	I'm not trying to deprive her of bragging rights for the coming onslaught of pain and nausea. I'm just trying to be supportive.
LISTENER:	*Your job is over.*
MARK:	See. And here I was crazy enough to think you'd say something shocking like "congratulations."

Little did I know that I would, in fact, share quite royally in the oncoming pain and nausea. That life-defining moments were merely hours away and that I should have felt ZERO guilt at Kaysie's desire for me to use the word "we." I was definitely going to earn this pronoun.

And it was, indeed, Kaysie who wanted us each to say "we." She has always been very sharing and inclusive that way. To this day, I intentionally make our couple statements mutual:

"We are pregnant."
"We homeschool our children."
"We don't say things like that."
"We beat we at Scrabble."
"We are feeling a little crampy this afternoon."

You see how it works.

"We are having a baby" became the favorite phrase. It was immediately followed by the favorite pastime: naming the baby. I work in creative circles, and creative circles take their time with the branding of offspring. It is a trophy to have the infant with the most clever and fitting moniker. This is why Gwyneth has Apple. This is why Julia has Phinnaeus and Hazel. This is why the process of elimination began that very early morning on the last of October. We instantly made out our initial "maybe" and "never" lists:

MAYBE	NEVER
Victoria	Bruce
Alyne	Sarge
Morgan	Dolly
Dawn	Peter
Colin	Lollygag
Ian	Kierkegaard
Jackson	Munch
Toben	Swollen
Reuben	Claus

My wife was especially fond of Reuben, but withdrew it from the list when we named a dog Reuben and he died within minutes.

However, there was plenty of time, because this was only the first morning. The wee hours of the morning, in fact. There would be plenty of time to celebrate and to create new, unheard-of names when I arrived home from the camp I had to fly off to in a matter of hours. As much as we would have loved to be festive that same evening, I had a commitment to speak for three days at a church youth camp.

Ah. Church youth camp. The breeding ground for infection.

Celebration would not come swiftly.

FIFTH PAUSE
for important autobiographical information

I do not have definitive proof, but I am suspicious that I was the lead singer of what may very well have been the worst Christian rock band in history. This is acceptable, because we never pursued it as a career and yet unacceptable, as people paid to hear us. It was not the musicians' fault. My brothers Brad (drums) and Dav (lead guitar) were well accomplished and our unrelated bassist, Ronnie, was skilled as well as a chick-magnet. But I wrote the songs.

It was a Christian band. A contemporary Christian band. From the 1980s. Formerly Sword of the Spirit, we relabeled ourselves the edgier (circa 1986) Advance. Advance to what—we never established.

I played the keyboards. I repeat: the keyboards. I wore suspenders and a funny hat—and, oh yes, I wore a very thin leather tie with piano keys imprinted on it vertically. The piano keys were fluorescent green like a highlighter. I was saving up for the Yamaha candy-red handheld keyboard when the band collapsed. This was evidently so I could gyrate or stagedive while playing—again—the keyboards.

I did not play the keyboards very well. Not ever.

I played the keyboards as an excuse to be in the band. My older brothers had always been required to take me with them to the mall, and it only made sense that they were also obligated to include me in whatever career choice they pursued. I took a long, hard look at each instrument and asked myself which one had a sound that was timeless. I chose the synthesizer.

This is how Advance became the greatest thing to happen to my high school. In other universes, this would sound impressive. However, it must not be ignored that my high school—no, my school: kindergarten through twelfth grade—was a total of twenty-eight people.

Yes. Twenty-eight. The shortest month has more days every four years than we had students. Yet I loved it because we were all so close.

I graduated in a class of four. I was the valedictorian, or as I like to call it: "the top 25 percent of my class." I was the only male in my graduating class, which meant that I had to sneak out of school for fifteen minutes every day to purchase chicken biscuits for the girls. Our school newspaper was the size of a coupon. Our yearbook came out every three years. My ten-year reunion was at the back booth of a Mexican restaurant.

But, back in the eighties, for a few years, I was a bee-bop hero to those twenty-eight because I did, indeed, write the songs—stretching for earnest rock rhymes like "He will wait until the latter but it won't matter" as if I were today's Tom Sawyer High on Jesus. My song titles alone were the envy of the minor masses:

- "Born Survivor"
- "Drag"
- "Fun with Dick & Jane" (I wish I were kidding)
- "Walls of Justice"
- "The Backstreet Jive"

"Backstreet Jive" was the audience favorite for no apparent reason. It was the lamest, most obvious C, F, G progression in history. We were energetic and frenetic on stage, but so is a possum who has just been hit by a car.

In 1988, the song took a tragic turn for the worst when a playful live aside transformed the bridge into "The Backstreet Rap." Lord, help us. Between that descent into delirium and our metal-anthem "Madder Than Hell," I don't know why we weren't struck by lightning and raptured right then and there while performing for $75 at the Solid Rock Café.

But these reasons are not why I feel my contribution made Advance the worst of all time. I legitimately feel this because of a question a musicmajor (trust me—it's one word, not two) posed to me in college:

> MUSICMAJOR: "Backstreet Jive," "Walls of Justice," those are interesting titles. What are those songs about?

What are those songs about?

Not "What are the lyrics?" but "What are they about?" The problem was that I knew all of the lyrics. I had written the lyrics. I knew what phrases would elicit cheers from our specific crowd of twenty-eight. I knew what would make them laugh, and I knew what would sound correct. But I had no idea what the songs were truly about.

Oh, be certain: each and every song had key Christian phrases—"know God is alive," "standing on a liquid bridge over a lake of fire," and the like. But they didn't mean much of anything at all. It had not been my mission to make them mean anything. My mission had been to rhyme and to please and to be applauded and to be allowed to do so by my parents because the songs mentioned Jesus. My mistake was that I had assumed those pursuits would somehow lead to poignancy or art.

I was incorrect. Somehow, the maudlin and the popular meant just a little bit to so many that they actually meant nothing at all. So I loosened the suspenders and hung up the fluorescent tie. I began the search for new ways to communicate. New ways to startle others into reality. To shock them into thinking.

And I slowly began to slip out of my pop-induced paralysis.

I could hardly contain the excitement. I had spent two days speaking to high-school students: making them laugh and enjoying their company—but wishing desperately to be back in the arms of my honey, calling one another mama and papa. My patience was about to pay off as I was flying home the next morning. All I needed was a sound night of sleep in my private cabin. As should be obvious by now, that sound night did not come.

I withered and wheezed all night as my sinuses slowly became impacted by the family of phlegm nesting there. By the next morning, I was so clogged that my head was spinning and my eyes throbbed. When I blew my nose too hard, a high-pitched squealing sound would emanate from my ears, and all of the camp dogs would begin ramming their heads against the dumpster.

I needed medication quickly. Something to open what was clogged: a menthol rub, liquid plumber, a #2 pencil, anything. But I was going to miss my plane if I stopped at a drug store. The key was to get to the airport as quickly as possible and purchase something helpful there.

I returned the rental car and hurried to the ticket counter as fast as my legs would carry me.

MARK:	Heddo.
WOMAN:	*Excuse me?*
MARK:	Heddo. Good mordig.
WOMAN:	*Can I get an interpreter over here?!*
MARK:	I'b sbeakig Eglish! By head is stobbed ub!
WOMAN:	*I'm sorry, sir, I can't understand you.* *Your head seems to be stopped up.*
MARK:	I'b goig to Tulsa.
WOMAN:	*And what is the flight number?*
MARK:	Flight dide wud sebed dide.
WOMAN:	*9179?*
MARK:	That's what I said. Dide wud sebed dide.
WOMAN:	*You don't seem to be feeling well.*
MARK:	Dot ad all.
WOMAN:	*Well, there's an earlier flight to Tulsa* *than 9179.*
MARK:	You're kiddig!
WOMAN:	*It's boarding right now. If you run, you* *can make it!*

And run I did. Like the wind. Along the way, developing that cold, clammy flop sweat one builds when exerting oneself with a fever. I arrived at the gate, feeling exhausted and imminently collapsible. I threw my ticket at the check agent and melted into my seat.

It was not until we began taxiing down the runway that it dawned on me that I had not purchased anything to unclog my head. I began to panic, but then realized that I had never personally experienced extreme altitude with clogged nasal passages myself. Perhaps the pain I had heard of that accompanies this sort of a situation was nothing more than an exaggeration. An urban myth. Like the geek on *The Wonder Years* growing up to become Marilyn Manson. Not true, just blown out of proportion. And then, a funny thing happened as we hit cruising altitude.

Life as I knew it ended.

The altitude and the pressure inside my head began to turn my ears into shaken bottles of soda. I curled into the fetal position and came close to weeping.

When we landed, Kaysie was at the airport with signs and balloons, the whole kit and caboodle. She was anticipating our celebration. But, when I walked off the plane, all I could do was cradle my ears with my hands.

Our celebration was postponed.

I continued to cradle my ears for the next twenty-four hours as I nursed the virus myself while on a production shoot. Whatever was going on in my ears finally produced enough pain to prompt nausea. I threw up my noon tabouli (probably why I'm still not all that excited about tabouli) and called Kaysie, telling her something was definitely wrong. She conceded to postpone our celebration again and picked me up to drive me to the emergency room.

The drive was the longest ten-mile excursion of my life. Every time we would pass by a car blasting the low end of some otherwise entertaining hip-hop confection, my ears would pulse and throb. I was practically on the floorboard of the automobile. We waited with approximately two other individuals in the emergency waiting room for more than an hour. As inexplicable as this is to the part of our brain known as "reason," try staring around the room in bewilderment while your eardrum is in a vise.

I have also learned a trick.

It's an interesting trick. When the waiting room attendant says, "The doctor will see you now," here's the trick:

She's kidding.

It's all a big joke for the medical staff to enjoy later. Because you see, the doctor does not see you now. You are, instead, ushered to a second, smaller, less comfortable waiting room where you will wait another lengthy period of time in private while browsing *Highlights for Children*, a reading magazine designed to entertain children who cannot yet read.

Kaysie repeatedly entreated the nursing staff for some sort of pain killer as I was emitting moans without realizing it. The staff resisted, wanting to identify the problem before subjecting me to something as radical as ibuprofen. Finally, the doctor entered (or so I assumed as I was cradled so low, I could only recognize her comfortable shoes) and placed on a rubber glove. This was evidently in case anthrax shot out of my ear in syringe form.

DOCTOR:	*There, there. Everything will be fine.*
ME:	Unnnnngh.
KAYSIE:	I've never seen him in so much pain.
DOCTOR:	*Yes, yes. Uh huh.*
KAYSIE:	No, really. He never responds like this.
ME:	Mmnnnm.
DOCTOR:	*No one ever does.*
KAYSIE:	It's worse than you think. I don't understand why he can't have pain killers.
DOCTOR:	*He'll be fine. This happens to children all the time—Oh!*

That is the moment she actually looked inside my ear.

She literally winced (or so I am told). She then took a second look. And a third. Evidently, there is some rule that each time you look at an infected ear, you have to push the cold, sharp, plastic triangular scope further into the drum itself. This advances the healing.

DOCTOR:	*I'm sorry.*
KAYSIE:	You're sorry?
DOCTOR:	*This is much worse than I thought.*

KAYSIE:	Yeah. That's why I said it was worse than you think.
DOCTOR:	*This eardrum is shriveled up like a raisin. It is about to fall out.*
KAYSIE:	Out?
DOCTOR:	*I'm afraid he's in a lot of pain.*
KAYSIE:	How much pain?
DOCTOR:	*Well—what he is feeling right now is comparable to childbirth.*

Childbirth. Out my ear.

So, due to the extremity of the pain, I was asked to remain for an additional forty-five minutes while another doctor was summoned. I was then given a prescription that would have to be taken across town to be filled. (Do they no longer have any drugs in the emergency medical facility itself? What if someone happened to have an actual emergency?) There I sat for an excruciating additional hour while whispering "happy place" and rocking back-and-forth in my seat to the drugstore Muzak version of Chumbawamba.

When the narcotic mix of numbing eardrops and painkiller-by-mouth finally kicked in, I literally collapsed across town at my brother's apartment, only partially cognizant of the concerned lamenting of Kaysie, my brother Dav, and his fiancée, Laura.

DAV:	*What happened?*
KAYSIE:	I don't know. We've hardly had time to talk since he got home from work.
LAURA:	Have you been able to celebrate yet?
KAYSIE:	No. Not yet.
DAV:	*What did you find out at the doctor?*
KAYSIE:	That I definitely don't want to have this baby out of my ear.

DAV:	*At least he's out of pain.*
KAYSIE:	I'm still concerned.
DAV:	*Why?*
KAYSIE:	He flies out again on Friday.

This was a concern for both of us. What would happen if my head remained clogged when I climbed on *another* plane to *another* high altitude? Would the eardrum actually fall out? Would my head implode? These were the questions for our family practitioner, who told me to rest assured. He would prescribe me something strong. Something that would cause the altitude to no longer be a problem. His only adamant guideline was that I wait and take the medication *the moment the plane was about to take off.* This was calming and a little bit frightening.

So Kaysie had the prescription filled, and I kept it safe and secure in its little narcotic Happy Meal paper sack fastened with a staple—waiting for that moment when I would be seated on the plane and the engines would rev up.

The moment of truth came. I had my bottle of water. The flight attendant told us to secure our safety belts, and I broke the staple seal, retrieving what I assumed was going to be pills. But it was not, in fact, pills. It was nasal spray. Certainly, nasal spray is not daunting if one is familiar with nasal spray. But I was not at all familiar with nasal spray. The dosage. The force with which I should snort. Could the fluid go too far into the back of my throat—was that possible and, if so, would the stewardess be any help? The plane was lurching forward. I had no time for research—only a sense of urgency that my window of safety was dissipating. I fumbled for the easy-to-read instructions on the bottle itself:

Take two snorts three times daily in each nostril twice.

No! No! No! These are not instructions! This is an SAT question! I began to panic. *I am confused! I will lift off into the sky unmedicated! What is a snort? Is it a sniff or a snore or in between? Do I multiply three times daily by* *two times? Do I carry the six?! We are lifting off the ground, and my happy place is still down there on the tarmac! The pain, the gnawing, the vise will be back! I cannot cannot cannot **will not** go through that again!*

So I chugged it nasally.

Perhaps an eighth of the bottle. *Oooh. How nice. Nasal spray gives a slight tingling, burning sensation.*

And just as the plane took off—so did I.

All of a sudden, I was floating above the other passengers as the stewardesses were flinging daisies. I was more than comfortable. I was in that warm place where flannel meets NyQuil. No more discomfort. An in-flight utopia where complimentary peanut servings were bigger and friends and relatives waved at the end of a long, bright tunnel.

The next thing I knew, the plane had landed in Atlanta, Georgia, and my friend was waiting to pick me up. I edged my way off the plane, walking like Katherine Hepburn talks. It was clear to Mitch (the friend) from my appearance that I was not feeling hunky-dory.

MITCH:	*Mark?*
MARK:	Motch!
MITCH:	*It's Mitch.*
MARK:	Mitchum. Morchum. How are that and you?
MITCH:	*Are you all right?*
MARK:	I'm falbulum. I have nose sprayed.
MITCH:	*Are you on some sort of medication?*
MARK:	The bestest sort.
MITCH:	*You look a little tired.*
MARK:	Do I? I did not notice. I have not seen my eyes lately. Where is Mortimer?
MITCH:	*Who's Mortimer?*
MARK:	My complimentary bag of peanuts.
MITCH:	*You can say "complimentary," but you can't say "Mitch"?*

MARK:	Foshizzle, my Mitchell.
MITCH:	*I almost didn't recognize you.*
MARK:	Really?
MITCH:	*I mean, behind all that drool.*
MARK:	It's my new look.

The medication did, eventually, wear off—giving me a mild headache and a craving for Pringles. But there was no time to stop for munchies as Mitch and I were late for the conference I was speaking at the next afternoon. Tonight, we would watch before taking part tomorrow.

So we wound up standing on the edge of the balcony as the live band kicked into worship. This being a youth convention, there was a great deal of energy and noise, and it was doing wonders for the clearing of my head. I felt as if I had completely regained my senses as those on stage launched into the first chorus: a song I was familiar with and, therefore, began to sing along:

MARK:	Jesus, you are Lord.
	Jesus, I love you.
	Jesus, you are flownin pownin.

Your assumption is correct.

That is not, in fact, the lyric to that song. Jesus is not, in fact, *flownin pownin.* I knew it was not the lyric to that song. I was attempting to sing the correct lyric to that song. My brain thought it. My mouth attempted it. But it was not the lyric that actually came out.

MITCH:	*What did you just say?*
MARK:	Did I jeb say flownin pownin?
	I did! I jeb sed flownin pownin!
MITCH:	*Are you all right?*
MARK:	I cabbot fide my tug.

This was accurate. I could not find my tongue. It had been there, in my mouth, moments ago. But now, search as I might, I found myself unable to discover its whereabouts. This, as you would expect, was not due to its actual disappearance, but rather due to the fact that everything behind my lips went suddenly and completely numb. My tongue lay there, dormant and motionless, like an infant in too much winter clothing.

It remained that way for a solid and terrifying ten minutes. No feeling whatsoever. I could have gnawed my tongue off and only been aware of it due to the taste. My mind wandered into a dissection of all the possibilities. How was this plausible? What could I have possibly done to trigger such a ...

Oh my word.
I have overdosed on nasal spray.

My mind ran rampant: Does this make me a junkie? Will this freeze if someone slaps me on the back like mother told me would happen when my eyes are crossed? Will I ever feel sensation in my mouth again? If I don't, does this actually make me funnier?

But, ten minutes later, I regained all feeling, and the crisis seemed over. I rejoined the worship session, singing all of the things that Jesus actually is and apologizing to Him for insinuating He was a flownin pownin, which means absolutely nothing and was filled with good intentions.

You may have noticed that I said "seemed" in the first sentence of the previous paragraph. This was due to the fact that I attempted to sleep off the numbness at the hotel overnight, considering it nothing more than a momentary flight of fancy. When I awakened, however, I jumped to an altogether different conclusion.

I woke up the next morning abruptly. *Very* abruptly. It was as if my eyes were open even before I gained complete consciousness. The room was very bright, and my mouth tasted like it does when one presses the tongue against a nine-volt battery, which I do not recommend.

I wander over to the mirror to assess what was causing these strange sensations. The answer is obvious as I discover that my left eye won't CLOSE.

WILL.
NOT.
CLOSE.

It is staring wide. Completely wide like Pavarotti's mouth at the end of "Ave Maria." To overcompensate, my right eye is attempting to force the left one closed by blinking furiously and uncontrollably. To make matters worse, my right nostril is circular and pronounced while my left nostril is hangdog and drooping. The right corner of my mouth is pinched while the left side is literally agape, hanging open without control and drooling all over the faux shag rug.

In short, the left side of my face is paralyzed.

And I go on stage in two hours.

I stare (not that I have any choice) into the mirror. How is this possible? Is there any sort of warning on the bottle of nose spray? There has to be some sort of mistake. And yet, as I tell my muscles to make things move, I *feel* them moving, but no motion actually occurs.

Well, this is clearly just nonsense, I tell myself. This is a momentary freak of nature. This will work itself out shortly. In the meantime, I will go on stage and do comedy anyway.

Certainly, no one will notice.

Earlier, when I listed my strangest onstage experiences, I may have made one glaring omission. I may have forgotten to mention the time that I performed for two thousand people with half of my face frozen.

In my performance history, I have indeed made audiences laugh, cry, cheer, and boo. I've made them listen in silence, and I've made them walk away. But I had never before that day frightened them with my appearance.

I weaved the way through my act while slurping, drooling, and blinking them into startled group insecurity. I was suddenly the special-needs comedian causing the younger children to soil themselves. But I bludgeoned my way through the act anyway. Perhaps it would have been easier for the crowd to swallow if I had actually mentioned the cause of my current state of appearance. But I thought that might draw undue attention.

So, I fly home the next morning. It is Sunday, and Kaysie is finally

153

expecting to celebrate the instigation of our little family. Instead, to her shock and chagrin, I exit the plane as Quasimodo.

KAYSIE:	*Stop doing that.*
MARK:	I'b dot doeeg it on burbose. I woke ub dis way yesterday.
KAYSIE:	*You what?!*
MARK:	Did I foged to tell you? I oberdosed od dasal spray.
KAYSIE:	*Honey—nasal spray can't do that.*

Panic sets in. The celebration will have to wait.

Monday morning, the doctor confirms that the dilemma has nothing to do with nasal spray, but rather the head virus mixed with the nasal infection caused a part of my brain to shut down. I have a condition called Bell's palsy—which sounds more like a carnival than a problem—and my face is indeed paralyzed.

Facial paralysis.

The doctor informs us that a certain type of drug could possibly cause a change resulting in normalcy that will take two weeks to two months. But, if that does not work, a more intense drug would be implemented, and it could take up to two years to be able to move.

But, there are, of course, some cases of Bell's palsy where the problem never gets any better.

We were floored. And confused. *What do you mean, never change? This has to change. I have a career, and it involves my face. You are wrong, Doctor! You are wrong. Why would God make me good at something just to take it away because of a head cold I contracted while doing what He made me good at doing?*

The immediate concern was my left eye. It was not closing at all, and this was an enormous danger. If the eye dried out, I would lose it completely. I was given artificial tears that I was to use several times per hour in order to keep the eye alive. I was also given the task of blinking my left eye by hand every few seconds as long as my face was paralyzed.

MARK:	Ebery few segonds?
DOCTOR:	*Unless you would prefer to lose the eye.*
MARK:	Ebery few segonds would be fide. Let be just jot dat down id by daytiber.

The doctor gave me heavy medication. Three days passed. No change. He increased the medication to a strong steroid. It is my belief that the steroid dosage was too much because overnight, my pectorals morphed into a duck that was cursing me in the French language.

The doctor put me on a lesser dose.
Weeks passed.
Nothing.

Our doctor spoke with other doctors and brought us into his office again. He had attempted every option in regard to medication—and every option had failed. *But, don't worry,* he insisted, *there's always brain surgery.*

Oh Lord God Almighty. How does something like this happen? Did I do something wrong? Am I going to stay like this forever? Do you want me to stay like this forever?

Kaysie and I would pray and discuss, and then alternate crying and laughing. We would cry because of the problem, and then laugh because I looked so stupid crying.

But this was truly perplexing. Here we were: people of faith. And the very thing I thought God wanted to use—that very thing is what is shut down. I don't mean to insinuate that I'm the best-looking individual in the world. It isn't that. It's just that I am a communicator by trade, art, and ministry, and that the face has to be utilized. The mouth, the intonation, the expression.

I mean, take comedy alone. How on earth would I continue to do the one-liner, the dumbshow, the pratfall. It's rarely the joke itself that is the stunner—the moment that gets the laugh. It's that unexpected shock right after the joke. The look. The loss of decorum. When the first guy begins to say something that seems so ordinary, so the second guy begins to take a sip of his drink—but what the first guy has to say is not ordinary at all—it is actually quite shocking. So the first guy says or does that thing—but he doesn't get the laugh or the audience reaction. The laugh comes from the second guy. Because when the first guy says or does that unexpected thing— that golden moment—the second guy loses it. He doesn't hold it in. He doesn't remain calm. He explodes. And thanks to that sip of drink, we see that explosion. It goes absolutely everywhere. That moment we, as humans, hold back but wish we could let loose. The uninhibited response to the unexpected—to the golden moments. To just let the liquid fly. It is called the spittake.

And how would I ever do it again when the face that is designed to so surprisingly respond is frozen shut?

Or perhaps—

Could that be why the face is frozen shut? Because I

have not been responding with abandon and surprise? Could the face that used to be so fresh and startling now be nothing more than rehearsed choreography? Could that be why it is frozen? Because it has numbed and succumbed to lethargy due to the lack of practice?

Certainly I have performed the rehearsed moves of the face. But how long has it been since those motions were fresh and natural—and surprising (even to myself)? Because there is life in that sort of abandon. In that sort of throwing-caution-to-the-wind. There is life there. And my face is dead—my vision in threat of being plucked out due to dryness. Like some sort of abandoned song lyric that doesn't really mean anything.

If my face is that out-of-practice from staying truly alive, perhaps my life is as well. Perhaps my faith is.

Have I grown lethargic and rehearsed in that which moves me? Have I not attempted to be rattled, surprised, and willing to lose decorum? Or have I memorized the motions of a spittake so well that I haven't actually felt the spittake in a very long time?

It became clear to me. My face was so easily able to give in to the paralysis because I had not exercised it. I had fooled myself into believing exercise was taking place, because I knew what exercise should look like.

But I had been resisting any sort of state of shock. Why? In fear of what I might look like if I lost decorum and wore the moment on my sleeve? Concerned at my appearance?

It didn't matter any longer. Because that appearance had been shot—not by the surprise or shock—but rather by the resistance to ever be moved.

And now the spit that could have so easily shot from my mouth in a moment of comic fury—that very spit was trickling down unfettered from a drooping, numb lip that I could no longer control.

chorophobia
THE MISUNDERSTOOD ARTIST

The description of the spittake may not sound very distinguished, but it is actually quite invigorating. In all my years in theater and improvisational comedy, I have never discovered a performer who did not thoroughly enjoy the experience.

I have also never discovered a performer who initially wanted to give the spittake a try.

You see, actors have a thing about appearances. Their livelihood is completely dependent upon the perception of others (where most occupations rely upon reality). That is why it is so complicated and so difficult for a performer to keep his or her life in balance. We are told not to need the acceptance of others, but we cannot gain or keep jobs without winning this acceptance. We are told applause is unhealthy while knowing full well that the lack of it is even more unhealthy because bills will not be paid. To the outside world, an actor being consumed with how he or she is presented may seem like pride while it is truly desperate survival. When successful, this usually becomes pride, and the vicious cycle continues.

This is why 99 percent of all performers are nothing more than average. They have an inherent resistance to appearing bad or weak or taken off-guard. But it is this exact vulnerability that turns an average performer into a world-class performer when he or she finally ceases to resist. The willingness to fall, to cry, to shockingly spit. This is what makes the act real—not *seem* real—but actually real. When a performer fears reality blending into his art but takes the leap there anyway, this makes a moment true. And when that which is true is actually worth performing, the moment will change both the audience and the artist.

This is what holds most performers back. It is called chorophobia or, in short: the fear of dancing. Not a fear of *choreography*. Believe me. There is a distinct difference.

Choreography is the dance that is planned. No one trained to dance fears a dance that is planned. Yet so many—even those who love to dance—fear the dance of the spontaneous moment, the dance of life. The willingness to aggressively and with great abandon follow as life and God lead. To be the improvisational partner, leaning entirely on the other as the dance progresses. It is the risky choice. The dance that is so frightening and so satisfying and may turn the corner to disaster at any given moment because, despite the fact that we are flexible and passionate, *we do not know what step will come next.*

This is the dance that we fear.

Had I put my true vulnerable feelings to music, my singular rock band experience could have been moving rather than maudlin. I believe there were one or two times when I actually did such a thing, but the songs were what I called *personal*. I played them for a few friends or family and never allowed them out of my arsenal of feelings again. I was proud of them because I dared to put what I felt on my sleeve—but what good did it do anyone when the sleeve was on a shirt that I never wore?

But it is not just my art that suffers here. I see a life lived long avoiding any fashion of spittake. As I have grown older, I have seen a building resistance to this sort of abandon inside and outside of myself. I gain experience and aptitude in what I do, how I perform, *who I am* as a person—as a follower of Christ—and I don't know that I get *better* as much as I get *used to it all*. That familiarity does not breed contempt, as some say. It breeds paralysis.

My face did not freeze because I did something daring. It became paralyzed because when sickness came calling, the face shut down and did not have the capacity to recall what it should do to jump-start itself. My face had become so complacent in *continuing* that it could not remember how to *begin* again.

Is this, in fact, what caused resistance to our message in Romania? Many blame failed outreach on the faith—making it as if the belief is unreal. But, perhaps, it isn't unreal. Perhaps the problem is that the faith is rote. Habitual and stale. Automatic motions and words. Saying and doing the *right* thing instead of the *good* thing. Caring about numbers instead of people. Perhaps the feeling left a long time before the obvious paralysis set in.

So, then the argument begins concerning feeling. I do not believe that following Christ is *about* feeling. But I do trust that a lived-out faith in God is about our response, both tangible and intangible. I believe the response can appear the same on the outside whether it is actual or manufactured. And I believe that the condition of the heart that chooses between those two options includes true feeling in its decision. I believe that the thief of our spiritual feeling is not disillusionment, as so many would insinuate. I believe the thief is the guarded protection of others' perceptions of ourselves. That in abandon lies attempt. In attempt lies discovery. In discovery lies true feeling. And in true feeling lies real ministry.

If I were not afraid for God to startle me—if I were willing to react to that astonishment naturally, regardless of how it made me appear—who knows how alive my mind and heart and faith would indeed become? But would I dare banish caution or pride or whatever I call it on that particular day and risk this?

I honestly do not know the answer.

But, oh—to make the attempt. The method is what I naturally resist, while the outcome is what I inherently crave. *The connection.* Knowing for a moment that I dared something I feared and that it mattered to someone else. That I revealed the skeleton—not in the closet—but the more painful one underneath the skin. And that it produced change in someone.

The artist in me,
the writer in me,
the minister in me—they love that.
And they are frightened by that.

That for me to feel alive, to bring life to others, I must risk being the fool or the failure or at least feeling the pain.

So, to find the answers to this future, I again revisit the past and take a long, hard look at that which prompted my face to once again move. The answer did not come where I expected that it would. Nor was it pleasant. In fact, the answer that triggered my healing just happened to have come from some of my inner fears.

Fears that I would be required to face if I ever wanted to set my world into motion again.

shocking the fool
THE FOOL IN QUESTION IS THE AUTHOR

It seemed to be a present of some sort.

My father set it down in front of me. There were three identical boxes. Wine-colored artificial leather. One box for each of the three oldest brothers. Each was fastened by what appeared to be a tiny gold latch with a fanciful letter "L" embossed just above it. I attempted to hedge my anticipation—but deep down, I knew presents that come in identical threes cannot be good.

It wasn't an actual present, per se, as much as it was the gift of opportunity. This was the way my father put it, and he could be extremely persuasive. We would be grateful, he continued, that he had made such an investment—even though it would take some effort on our part—when we were grown and wealthy beyond our wildest imaginations.

My dad didn't know that the wealth in my wildest imaginations went pretty high up there and that I always felt a little bit guilty for even dwelling on such magnanimous pleasures.

I had always considered wealth an instant possibility— available at any moment or whim if luck or God hit the wind just right. Part of this was due to Dad's theory that if I took just one dollar and had a bank double the total every day, I would be a millionaire in a very short period of time. Mathematically, this was both accurate and astounding. I was simply unable to locate the bank that would actually do this daily doubling based upon the deposit of one dollar—but I was still looking.

But there were other ways to beat the system, and one of the best seemed to be these three identical boxes. My father eloquently built up the mysteries of prosperity hidden inside, just waiting to be unlocked. My father had steered me right many times and made many sacrifices for me, so I watched in rapt attention as he handed the reins over to another, well-dressed man who appeared suddenly and mysteriously out of our kitchen.

We were told that our lives were about to change. Certain fortune was upon us. Because we were one of "very few families" selected to test-market a new concept, called a downline, where we would benefit from other poor schmucks selling beneath us while we, in fact, schlepped for those above us—namely our parents.

Yes! We were some of the lucky few who were given the opportunity to shell out thirty bucks per box to own our very own samples that would prompt frenzied consumer sales! We would be the envy of all neighbors, and any and all who wanted in on the scheme would be forced to join our (MOOHAHA) doooownliiiine! Eventually (within days, it was portrayed), we would never have to sell another item, never lift another finger. There would probably be no need to actually finish high school.

Why?! Because we would be the pioneers! The entrepreneurs who realized that our lives and the lives of those above us could all be changed quickly and painlessly!

How?

By going door-to-door and selling tiny bottles of fake crappy cologne imitations out of a cheap, embossed box.

DAAAAD! I hate selling!

You'll sell it, and you'll like it. *Dad is an engaging, enigmatic man whom I love, and somehow he made this sound both positive and mandatory. Though I knew deep down that I would neither sell well nor like it at all.*

So—though I had experienced futility in all previous family sales efforts: the overpriced candy bars, the coupon books, the lotions, the powdered spinach vitamin supplements—I thought I would give this new, clearly superior product a college try.

There are suckers born every minute. Hopefully, they lived within biking distance and were not already in someone else's downline.

BRAIN SURGERY?! I can't possibly undergo brain surgery! There has to be something else that will motivate my face to move again!

The doctor paused to stare at me—the sort of stare one might utilize to determine one's mettle, or to size up the next fresh kill. The wheels were clearly turning as if he were struggling to even make the suggestion.

DOCTOR:	*There is one way.*
MARK:	Dere is?!
DOCTOR:	*But you're not going to like it.*
MARK:	Dogter, if it will figz by face, I will lub id.
DOCTOR:	*There is a process that we have not attempted that may very well kick-start your face.*
MARK:	Kigztart?
DOCTOR:	*Yes.*
MARK:	Why duz dat sound like yer goig to use jumber cables?
DOCTOR:	*Because the process to which I am referring is called shock therapy.*

Shock therapy. As in electric bolts shooting into my face.

There were many rules in our house growing up that I deemed "foggy," or at least they were nonspecific enough that I could explain the crime away as a misinterpretation. I knew deep down that I shouldn't dig newly sharpened pencils through the shag rug, but that didn't keep me from getting graphite embedded into my left hand where it remains visible to this day. However, where many rules remained open to interpretation, shooting electrical currents into my face was not one of those. Electrical safety regulations were seared upon my gray matter.

- Don't play with Mister Microphone in the tub.
- A coat hanger should never touch where the lightbulb goes.
- Lando Calrissian's left foot does not belong in the electric socket.

I was an obedient boy, and I wanted to LIVE, so I kept all of my appendages as far away from the outlets and currents as possible. I maintained this regimen, even into adulthood, until the day my doctor told me that I would need to intentionally electrocute myself in order to regain face.

MARK:	How egzackly would dat work?
DOCTOR:	*I'm not at liberty to say.*
MARK:	Yer dot ad liberdy?
DOCTOR:	*But I know a guy down the road.*
MARK:	A guy dowd da road?
DOCTOR:	*Yeah. He specializes in this sort of thing.*
MARK:	Is he goig to sell by spleen to drug traffickers?
DOCTOR:	*No. It's a hospital facility down the road.*
	Here is his card.
MARK:	Andy Tanderson: Shock Therapist.
DOCTOR:	*Trust me.*

I won't do it. I won't stand inside the doorjamb of the house while she goes to the basement to get her checkbook. Why would I need to stand inside the house? And what kind of a freakazoid keeps her checkbook in the basement? I decline, and she angrily slams the door as I lose yet another potential sale of what I have been instructed to call "imitation," but I know deep down are "fraudulent," perfume copies.

This bites. It really does.

My chain keeps popping out of my stupid bike, and I have to balance this seven-pound leatherette sample box on my handlebars. I've stuffed the order sheet and the pencil down my pants, which not only makes the form crumpled but puts me in a precarious position for pedaling. I already have a graphite pencil point stuck in my hand. I don't want one anywhere else.

If I could just get one sale, *I could go home and watch CHiPs. The reruns just started showing in the afternoon. Oh the fickle hand of fate, handing me this box just as Jon and Ponch launch into syndication!*

Do you want some perfume?
How much is it?
Eight dollars.
For that tiny bottle?
No. That's the sample. The bottle's much larger, and if you pay me right now, you will receive it in ten to twelve weeks.
No thank you.
I'll give you my bicycle.
SLAM!

Urngh! The theme music. The theme music had to be starting right now—the part where the camera zooms over the city and then somehow magically swoops down to the interstate just as the California Highway Patrol motorcycle team rides by. The camera gets tighter and tighter till we see the WHEELS! As close as the WHEELS, man! That ROCKS, and it's on RIGHT NOW, and I HAAATE people who want to smell good!

I taste one of the sample bottles of perfume. I actually put some of it in my mouth. I reason that it might be cool to tell the guys at school that I did this.

Maybe it's the episode where they raise money for polio by roller skating with Todd Bridges. That one's not very good. Nothing explodes. I'm not missing much if it's that one.

Hello, sir. I'm trying to raise money by selling these
inexpensive cologne replicas.
Raise money for what?
For me to spend.
I don't use cologne.
But you would if it were only eight dollars, wouldn't
you?
Eight dollars? For that tiny bottle?
IT'S A SAMPLE! FOR CRYING OUT LOUD! GEEYA!
Do you have a permit for that?
I don't need one.
Everyone needs one.
My dad said it was okay.
You live around here, kid? I'm calling the cops!

*I bolted. I left my bike in the street and bolted. I knew I
would double back for it, but I would do it nonchalantly,
as if I were just happening back in the direction of the
churlish neighbor's house. For the moment, though, I
would just sit inside the shrubbery next door and stare.*

Not the cops. Cops were bad.

Except for Jon and Ponch, of course.

    I am seated in the waiting room of some sort of medical clinic with
no signs out front. No labels whatsoever. Just a blank lobby with a single
receptionist desk where no one is seated. However, there is another,
unmarked door beyond the desk.
    I walk through that door and am told that I am not supposed to be in
there. I protest that there is no one out front. I am informed that this is
understood and that, if I will be patient, Physical Therapist Tanderson will

be with me in a few moments, Mr. Steele.

These people know who I am.

I close the door slowly and slip quietly back into my seat in the waiting area. I drum my fingers. I blink my eye with my hand every few seconds, as I have been doing for the past four weeks. My eye is now black-and-blue from all of this activity. I glance around. No magazines. Not even a *Highlights for Children*. Well, that makes sense. Children should not be here. Neither should I. I consider what types of magazines should be in the lobby of a shock therapist. *Psychology Today. Guns & Ammo. Cat Fancy.*

Just then, the door is thrust ajar. A thin, excitable man with a too-wide smile speed walks to me a bit briskly. He sits in the chair next to me and leans uncomfortably in.

ANDY: *HOWDY! You must be Mr. Steeley.*

He pronounces the silent "e." I hate that. I stare. Not that I have any other choice but stare.

MARK: My nabe is Thpftsteele.

He begins to laugh heartily.

ANDY: *YOU CAN'T SAY YOUR NAME!*
MARK: What?
ANDY: *Your face is so messed up, you can't say your name! That is hilarious!*
MARK: You bust be Dogtor Tanderthpfton.
ANDY: *Sh Sh Sh Nup Shup!*

He closes in even further and whispers.

ANDY: *Don't call me doctor. The real doctors hate that.*
MARK: You're dot a real dokter?
ANDY: *Heavens, no. I'm a shock therapist.*

MARK:	What's da differedce?
ANDY:	*School.*

He escorts me toward the back of the building and informs me that there is only a slight chance that my face will return to normal, but that he is going to give it his best shot and that I should not be uncomfortable while he stares at my face for a lengthy period of time. He wants to get to know the enemy that is my frozen visage.

Andy opens the door, and I enter a room with a small chiropractic table. It is the only furniture in the room, which is probably for the best, because 60 percent of the room is taken up by what appears to be an ice-rink zamboni humming like a nuclear plant.

MARK:	Whad ith zat?
ANDY:	*Don't even think about that. It's nothing.*
MARK:	Id's nutting? Den why izit takig ub so much thfpace?
ANDY:	*That's the power generator.*
MARK:	For da therapy?
ANDY:	*Don't ask. Don't tell.*

Physical Therapist Tanderson seems to know what he is doing, and he is making brave attempts to calm me, but I am a bit overwhelmed—both at his cheery persona and at the threat of impending electrocution. He stares and pokes and prods my face with his capped pen, jotting down notes. Then, sensing my trepidation, he attempts to explain what is about to happen to me in terms that the victim is able to understand.

ANDY:	*It's really no big deal. I'm just going to take these little electrodes that are attached to this big scary voltage-laden box and attach them to little places on your face. Now, calm down and put your hand in this water.*
MARK:	WAHDER?! ARE YOU IDSADE!

ANDY:	*It would seem so, wouldn't it? But, actually,*
	I'm just here to help. Unfortunately, this sort
	of help is associated with hot, searing voltage.
	So let's turn the machine on now, shall we? If the
	lights in the building happen to wane and flicker,
	that's a coincidence and completely unrelated.
MARK:	I'b dervous.
ANDY:	*Everyone's nervous their first time, Mr. Steeley.*
MARK:	Thpftsteele!
ANDY:	*Oh man. That never gets old. Yes, everyone gets*
	nervous. But, don't worry—with this size of a
	current, you'll eventually lose the part of your
	brain that acknowledges fear.
MARK:	Ekthcuthe me?
ANDY:	*A joke. To break the ice.*

But the ice was not broken. Despite numerous requests that I relax, I was having a difficult time remaining seated. Physical Therapist Tanderson continued to affirm that, though the experience would be a new and unique sensation, it was nothing I could not handle. My life was not in danger; I simply needed to prepare myself for what he called the bite.

MARK:	Da bite?
ANDY:	*Yes. See, most think the shock will hurt.*
	It doesn't hurt. It bites.
MARK:	Duzzent a bite hurt?
ANDY:	*I'll tell you in a minute.*
	First, let's crank up this power knob.
	Now, if you will just sit with your hands in your
	lap, I will take my little cattle prod and tap it to
	your face muscle in one, two, three—
	NOW!

Nothing. Absolutely nothing.

I open my one good eye to see Andy, staring with a puzzled expression on his face. The cattle prod is touching my cheekbone. The dial is turned up. The zamboni is humming.

But—nothing.

ANDY: *Well, uh—that's normal.*
             Just let me turn this round thing up a little more.
             What I meant to say was that you would
             eventually feel something on the second try,
             which is right NOW!

Nothing.

ANDY: *Not a bite?*
MARK: Doe.
ANDY: *Maybe a tingle?*
MARK: Doe.
ANDY: *Perhaps you remember a lost bit of trivia?*
MARK: DOTHING!
ANDY: *Well, that's normal.*
             If you never feel anything—that's normal.
             (But you should feel something.) How about—

NOW! (turn the knob) Nothing.
NOW! (turn the knob) Nothing.
NOW! (turn the knob) Nothing.

MARK: ADDY TADDERSUD?!
ANDY: *Well, that doesn't make any sense!*
             Just let me take a look at my cheat sheet here.
             What should happen is that if I place your hand
             here, and if I turn this knob like so, and if I press
             this against your muscle here, then there's
             no reason you shouldn't—

WHAM

POW!

Suddenly, I realized what a deer hit by a tractor-trailer felt like. My head kicked back horizontally, and my teeth fillings went hot. The blur of whiteness slowly faded from my vision, and there in the haze was Andy Tanderson, staring at me with both eyes as wide as my bad one.

ANDY:	*How did that feel?*
MARK:	Like a really big BITE!
ANDY:	*Well—well, that's normal.*
	That's the way it should be.
	I mean, you were gonna kick
	those shoes off anyway, weren't ya?
	Let me just pick those suckers right up.
	Well—this one's a little heavy—
	Ohp, there's a couple toes in there.
	And, hey—you look better with that
	white streak down your hair that children get
	when they've seen ghosts. So, we'll just get back
	to business, but first let me turn this knob
	back down a little.
MARK:	Whad—
ANDY:	*Hm?*
MARK:	Whad did you just say?
ANDY:	*Just a tad, really.*
MARK:	Why would you deed to terd id dowd a tad?
ANDY:	*A funny thing. I'll tell you later.*
MARK:	Tell me dow.
ANDY:	*When you didn't respond, I kept turning it up*
	little bit by little bit.
MARK:	How far did you terd id up?
ANDY:	*All.*
MARK:	**ALL?!**
ANDY:	*DON'T YELL AT ME!*
	IT'S YOUR FACE THAT'S STUPID!

So for the next half hour, Physical Therapist Andy Tanderson bit me with his cattle prod. Over and over, shock after shock, pain after pain. I felt twitches and tweaks and began to cling to a hesitant hope that this discomfort might lead to something.

The session ended, and I asked for a mirror. Andy refused to give me one because the healing would not be instantaneous. If I wanted to know if progress had been made, I would have to wait until morning.

But in the morning—not one thing had changed.

I stood over my bike in the middle of the street.

I glanced about. Eight, maybe ten houses I had never visited before were within sight. My CHiPs *window was dissipating, and I could not go home without at least one sale.*

WHY do I need to make a sale? This will amount to nothing. I don't want to be rich. I mean, I do, but I don't wanna look at these tiny bottles for one moment longer. I don't wanna be rich today.

But, which house? Who would actually buy this garbage? Which house looked gullible?

I stuck my finger out and spun in a circle.

Hello, Miss. Is your mother at home?
I am the mother of this home.
Well, you certainly wear the years well. I was across the street, selling my last few bottles of limited-edition discount popular fragrances when I thought I should

just check to see if perhaps you would like to place an order (at today's reduced rate) that will be filled as soon as more stock arrives.

Well, aren't you thoughtful?

Yes, ma'am.

How sweet. There need to be more young men like yourself.

I do what I can, Miss.

And you're a part of that family up the street with the van to that Christian school, aren't you?

What?

Is that a good school? Do you like it?

I—uh—um—oh.

You selling these for that school?

Kind of.

Well, I could use some perfume. Let me get my checkbook.

No.

No?

No. I'm not selling them for the school—actually. I'm— I'm just selling them for myself.

Because you like doing this?

No.

Then, why?

Because I want to make Dad happy.

You have to sell to make your dad happy?

NO! No. I just—want to make back at least as much money as he spent on this box.

How many have you sold?

None.

You haven't sold any at all?

I'm a pretty crappy salesman.
But, you just said ...
I lied.
Oh.

Sorry.

What are you sorry for?
I didn't tell you the truth.
Sure you did—eventually.
You shouldn't buy any. They're eight dollars, and you
won't get them for, like, five months—but you'd have to
pay me now.

How much did the box cost?
Thirty dollars.
How much profit do you get for each bottle?
Five of the eight.
*Here. I'll buy three, and then you're halfway there. Now,
your dad can be proud of you.*
I don't think the way I've done this would make him
very proud.

Well—I would disagree.

*She smiled as she shut the door. I looked down at my
hand. A check for twenty-four dollars. I was stunned
to realize that a fleeting moment of what could only be
described as honesty seemed to have unparalyzed my
stalled success. That being unguarded had been the
answer.*

More than stunned. It had shocked the fool out of me.
I looked at my watch.

CHiPs was almost over.

I decided to go try a few more houses.

Okay, God. This is it. What am I supposed to do with this?

Do with what? Your face?

YES! MY FACE! I am very confused here.

What exactly confuses you?

Well—I was under the impression here that I needed
my face for my calling—

You mean My calling?

Yes. That's what I meant. Your calling. I've tried everything—
I've been obedient—and You haven't healed me.

I see. How does that make you feel?

How does it make me feel?

That's right.

Confused.

That's all?

And a little bit angry.

A little bit.

Sometimes more than a little bit.

I am going to ask you a question now.

Go ahead.

Would you obey Me even if your face stayed frozen?

Of course
(but change it).

You do realize that it's not a punishment. There are rules.

Of course, I realize that. Which rules do You mean?

I have given you many gifts, like your face.
Your face is not the only thing frozen.

I understand that.

These gifts have to be worked out.

I do! I do that!

You do the same things over and over again.
That's not working things out. That's keeping things stale.
You can't allow something to fade away
and then be angry that it is gone.

But what about the miraculous?

I would be happy to bring you a miracle—
but what you asked for was to be fixed.

I don't understand. A miracle would fix it.

Certainly. But if you don't change, the same habits will lead
to the same paralysis all over again. If you want permanent health,
*then **you** have to change, Mark.*
For you to change, it will require a process
—not a miracle.

But miracles are quicker.

I understand.

And I look ridiculous.

You look like you're learning.

And there's danger involved.

There's always danger involved.
This time, I allowed you to see it.

This is a little bit shocking.

Moments of honesty always are.
So the question remains: Would you rather
have a quick fix or would you rather change?
Would you rather be fed miraculously while lost in the wilderness
or would you rather grow your own food in the land I have promised?

I would rather change quickly.

It's one or the other.

I can rescue you, Mark.

But I would rather change you.

Let your guard down.

Be a little shocked.

Let me work on the inside.

Allow the good to work its way out.

One week later, I paid a final visit to Physical Therapist Andy Tanderson. After my internal argument with God, I felt more accepting of Andy's eccentricities and allowed him to take his approach with little to no argument from me.

As I sat on his chiropractic table, getting stung bit by bit, I paused to ask him the question that had been rolling around in my mind: Why did he have to shock the muscles? Was it indeed like jumper cables juicing up a car battery?

No, he responded. He had to shock the face in order to remind those muscles that a face is indeed what they were designed to be.

The following morning after the second therapy session, I awakened to a sensation I had not felt in almost six weeks. My left eye was moist. I ran to the mirror.

I had been completely healed.

Kaysie and I were brought to tears. I thanked God for what had been accomplished—but mostly, I thanked Him for what I had been taught.

There were a few inconsistencies that had to be corrected with several months of therapy. The right eye, which had been blinking incessantly all this time, now needed a rest. It was overcompensating by remaining wide open when not blinking. To this end, the left eye drooped tired, causing my eyes to be a bit out of sync. The only way to equalize them was to open the left eye wide to match the right. This would not have been a problem this miraculous morning.

Except that this was the morning I was in my brother Dav's wedding.

To this day, a testament remains to the miracle accomplished in my life. It is in the living room of my brother's house. A group wedding photo. If you look closely, you will see me standing somewhere near the back.

I am the wide-eyed psycho staring you down.

But the wedding ended without a drooling Quasimodo in the party. And I became a new person with fresh wounds. The sort of wounds that remain partially open, waiting for God to startle and surprise, forever anxious for the next spittake.

Dav and Laura left for the honeymoon.

My parents went home to Atlanta.

And Kaysie and I finally celebrated our future beautiful baby girl with both eyes wide open.

5

*blood*LETTING

So, which is it?

Which is what?

Is this conversation between your left brain and right brain or between you and God?

You're a part of it. What do you think?

I think I'm confused.

That's what the conversation is for—
to stop the confusion.

But are you conversing with yourself or God?

A little bit of both, I think. Whatever God chooses to use best.

So, it's all God then?

No. My own voice gets in there a lot and messes things up.
But when I ask myself the tough questions and listen
instead of immediately deliberating, the answers tend to come.

Do you listen much?

I know I did at least once.

How do you know it was God that once?

Because I absolutely did not want to do what He asked me to do,
but I knew that I would do it. Somehow, I knew that I would.

the negative
A STORY WITH SUBTITLES

SIXTH PAUSE
for important autobiographical information

I am a very upbeat person. I consider myself—as far as encouragement to others goes—to be extremely positive. So, it was startling the morning in college when I discovered that at my very life source, I am the most negative of all.

I loathe and detest needles—not all needles, mind you. The ones that crochet sweaters have never done me any substantial harm. But the needles used for vaccinations and the like—they are the enemy.

I had vowed to stay far away from these devices as long as possible. This is why I suffered such disdain when I realized that there was a blood drive at my university and that they were paying cold hard cash.

"Lack of money" for a college student is only a fraction further down the list below activities involving needles. No needles meant no money, which meant no dates, which meant no future.

Needles win!

I made my way to the blood drive, anxious to deposit my withdrawal and leave with a few of those butter cookies you can actually stick onto your pointer finger. I had never given blood before, so it was required that I be tested. When the test was complete, the woman looked at my results and almost shouted her findings.

> *AB NEGATIVE!*

To the non-bloodworker, this means very little—but evidently, my veins had struck some sort of gold rush. AB Negative is an extremely rare blood type. I was congratulated and told that, though the blood was rarer than the others, I would still only receive the twenty dollars agreed upon.

I exited the building pinching a cotton swab on my sore arm and wearing three daisy-shaped cookies on my left hand. I sensed the irony: a positive individual with negative inside him. It seemed as rare as the blood type itself.

I wonder why they say it is so valuable. Perhaps one day, it will come in handy.

I believe that giving blood should always be intentional. Blood is a precious commodity and should not be wasted. I believe this partially because I now have a better understanding of how valuable blood is. But the other part of me believes this because I am clumsy and have given up too much of my own blood for no reason.

There is a Mexican city just over the border of El Paso, Texas, that I have traveled to fourteen times. A weathered city with beautiful people. It is called Ciudad Juarez.

The city is broken up into two sections: the tourist market area with restaurants, carnivals, and street beggars and the hidden Ciudad Perdidas or "lost city." Between these two locales, the majority of dwellers reside amidst churches and gangs.

I have led missions teams as small as a dozen and as large as forty into this city to minister, to bring medical and practical needs, and to accomplish building projects for a local orphanage. Through these fourteen missions, I have built lifelong relationships with the Mexican people, had my heart broken a dozen times over by their love and their need, and given massive amounts of accidental blood.

I don't know that it is the city itself that takes my blood as much as it is the fact that there are simply more incidents in this sort of environment through which one might be wounded.

One trip in particular was marred by three instances of severe flesh wounds. It began in the middle of the night as I lay restless in a sleeping bag on the frigid concrete floor of one of the orphanage classrooms. I had just reached that state of almost-comfort where one convinces oneself that, if one does not move, one may just be able to fall asleep in the current position. But my bladder needed emptying, so I took the jaunt into the darkness for relief. As I stepped into the bathroom, I realized that I would be unable to find the toilet without a light. I did not want to wake anyone, so I began to push the door closed. It would not budge. It seemed to be caught on something soft. So I gave it one last hard shove.

And felt something suspiciously hot.

I flicked on the light in a hurry to discover that the bathroom door was made of metal and that the bottom corner had been pulled upward, away from the frame, where it was now a jagged incisor of rust. I know for a fact that this edge was sharp enough to cut through skin. I know this because when I shoved the door open, it caught the top of my foot and filleted it open from stem to stern.

I stared as the top surface of my foot poured blood. I just stared.
I had just sliced my foot like a loaf of bread.
With a rusty door.
At three in the morning.
In Mexico.

This can't be good.

Fortunately, one of the men on our team was studying to be a nurse. I hoped he was at least far enough into the study to recognize gangrene. I would have normally assumed the best of a medical student's judgment, but this particular individual had toweled off all week with a small rubber shammy that smelled like homeless feet. I could not help but question his cleanliness.

The male nurse was summoned immediately. He surveyed the area while some servant-like missionary sopped up my blood with a T-shirt of Bart Simpson drinking tequila.

MALE NURSE:	*Hmm.*
MARK:	What does Hmm mean?
MALE NURSE	*This isn't too bad.*
MARK:	See, and here I thought the ability to see bone was a warning sign.
MALE NURSE:	*Does anyone have any super glue?*
MARK:	Are you kidding me?
MALE NURSE:	*No. It's sanitary.*
MARK:	Forget sanitary! Do I need stitches?
MALE NURSE:	*Very much. But you're not going to get any here.*
MARK:	Why not?
MALE NURSE:	*Do you want to go to a Mexican hospital?*

And the absolute truth was that as much as I loved and cared for these people and wanted the best for them, NO. I did not want to get stitches at the Mexican hospital. I had been OUTSIDE the Mexican hospital to minister. That was close enough. I came to this city to hurt for these people—to a certain limit. I would not be getting stitches this evening.

The male nurse created some makeshift pseudo-stitches by forging the skin folds of the wound together with bandages, twine, and what I believed to be electrical tape. There was also a great deal of antiseptic crème utilized. I bit down on something I thought was a belt but later reminded me of pet jerky treats.

There was a continual throbbing pain, but I remained capable of walking. This was good news, because the next day we were headed for the Lost City.

The circle had been created outside the building. It was our routine. We would arrive as a group of thirty-or-so, dressed in colorful costumes and makeup. We would round out an area with our sound system and equipment, and then we would split up into groups to welcome children, families, the homeless—anyone who seemed like they needed love.

I had brought so many groups on so many trips that I no longer wore the costumes myself. The contact, Jonatan, (who had become a close friend) and I would take care of all surrounding details while the others cut their teeth on outreach. It was a training ground for future missions leaders. They had a lot to learn. It was their turn to wear the funny costumes.

When the ministry time began, we would round up the locals with some upbeat music and eventually perform a short drama that would lead toward our ultimate message of a Savior who brings healing, who meets needs.

I watched the team begin. I looked up at our current location.

The Mexican Hospital.

As guilty as I felt for thinking it, I was glad I was not the one doing the drama.

I stood next to Jonatan and scoped the area for ministry opportunity. I eyed two women in their mid-thirties standing across the way, eyes fixed on the actor playing Jesus.

They were weeping, and the drama had just begun.

Yes. Those are the ones. That is who Jonatan and I will minister to.

That ministry will be painless.

Ciudad Perdidas is easy to miss. There are no road signs on the path to this village because road signs would require the city officials to admit that the city exists. If the city existed, power lines would have to be directed and water would have to be brought in. Unemployment percentages would skyrocket. No. There would be no sign directing the common passerby to Ciudad Perdidas. It would not be drawn on any of the official maps. One would have to be searching for it. Along the paved roadway that leads to legal tourist atrocities, just to the right veers a dust road. Follow it for two miles or so, and over the second hill, a sea of old refrigerator boxes with windows carved into them stands. As far as the eye can see, cardboard houses. Clouds of stirring dust. Thousands upon thousands of people living in abject poverty. And outside the cut-out windows, the inhabitants can see with their own eyes the tourists pouring into the spectacularly lit attractions and restaurants just across the dry riverbed.

The first time I stepped into the Lost City, it was a sobering experience. I knew now to remain quiet as we drove across its borders as God was inevitably working in the hearts of the others in our van. But now I had grown in affection for the people living here—especially the children. They had never known what they did not have and were, instead, joyous when we would arrive with gum and balloons, a bag of groceries for their parents, a football to toss around, and another chance for them to see the story of their Savior.

I would have to tread lightly this time around, as I had never trekked the hills of the Lost City with this sort of apparatus around my foot. I hobbled to where the children were kicking the ball around, hopping on my good leg as much as possible. The remnants of a garbage bag were wrapped about my wounded leg to serve as a sealant from the dust, grime, and elements.

In the spirit of sacrifice, I determined to not allow this challenge to affect my desire to play with the children. I tossed a ball to an eight-year-old. He reared back and threw me a pass. I lunged for it.

And felt something suspiciously hot.

My leg was caught. I groaned and winced as I recognized the feeling, but could not imagine under what circumstances this recent history could be repeating itself.

I glanced down toward my leg.

It was caught. Hung up on a three-foot, rusty metal spike that was sticking out of the ground for no apparent reason.

I had turned in such a way that it had caught just above my ankle and slit upward like a razor blade three-quarters of the way to my knee.

Wide open. Dirty. Pouring blood.

I wondered if perhaps the male nurse was nearby.

The drama concluded, and I motioned to Jonatan. This was the way it worked. A dozen trips and seven years later, we had our communication down to hand signals. Jonatan's code of gestures was slightly more complicated than mine in the single fact that his code changed every time he felt like it should. We would be driving with five lanes of Mexican automobiles squeezed into three lanes of dirt-road traffic, and he would motion for me to take

flash BANG

a right turn from the left-hand lane by stroking his nose briefly with his finger at the last second. This was what he considered fun.

But the jokes went on hold during ministry time, and Jonatan saw the same two hurting women across the way whom I had seen. We approached them together and inquired as to their sadness.

Despair. Hopelessness. Family suffering.
The desperate hope that there could possibly,
by some miracle, be a better life here on earth.
And if not here, in the hereafter.

We understood, not because we were aware of their status or history, but because we shared the same questions—the same needs.

For the next twenty minutes, Jonatan and I told them about our personal experiences with Jesus Christ and the relationship that has anchored and ruddered us through each and every storm.

We told them that Jesus brought us right here, right now to help them. They asked us to pray with them. But when the prayer was over, the tears did not stop.

This was not unusual, as many emotions come when an individual truly gives his or her life over to Christ. But that was not the type of tears we were witnessing.

This was deep sorrow.

Is there anything else?
Yes. It is our mother.
Is she in that hospital?
She is dying.
Your mother is dying?
Right here. Right now. And Jesus sent you to help us.

MALE NURSE:	*What did you do to your leg?!*
MARK:	I don't have the slightest idea!
	I just turned away from this kid,
	and my leg was on fire!
MALE NURSE:	*Does this sort of thing happen much*
	at home?
MARK:	Never.
MALE NURSE:	*Man, we gotta get you out of Mexico.*

Except that I did not want to get out of Mexico. I wanted to paste and duct tape my leg up the same way we did the foot. I wanted to leave a note apologizing for staining their sand street with my blood. I wanted to continue to help. But I wanted to do so without risking any more life and limb.

A few more days passed until it was almost time to drive across the border. I had survived forty-eight additional hours without injury through a mixture of hesitancy and continual protection: surrounded on all sides by college students searching to remove random sharp objects. From the waist down, I looked like King Tut, but I was resolved to finish the task at hand.

I had not been given a quiet moment to myself in days. It was beginning to drive me crazy. So, I snuck away from the group in order to clean the van. No one would notice that I was gone. I would certainly be safe.

In retrospect, I consider it an impossibility to have done anything about the third incident. I was simply cleaning a vehicle. Is that such a crime? Normally, I would have had faster reflexes. To my defense, both my leg and

flash BANG

foot were melded together with something only mildly stronger than arts and crafts paste.

I could have sworn that, previously in the week, the male nurse had not shown much athletic aptitude—but here he was, ignorant to the fact that I was lurking behind that van door. Here he was, hurling the football the single time he would throw it all week. Here he surprisingly had guns for forearms and catapulted that pigskin like there was no tomorrow. Here the recipient of his throw was incapable of catching said pass. Here I suddenly appeared from behind the van door just as the football came into view. Here the hardened corner of that football hit me full-force in the socket of my right eye. Here the power of the ball shoved my head briskly, ramming it solid into the door of the van. Here I lay on the concrete of Mexico with a black-and-blue eye and a lump where there was once only skull.

MALE NURSE: *Mark?*
MARK: What happened?
MALE NURSE: *You caught the football with your eye.*
MARK: I think my foot opened back up.
MALE NURSE: *That's it.*
We're leaving Mexico right now.

But we would not leave Mexico right now. Because there was a mission remaining.

We climbed the stairs back to the glue, the gauze, the ice pack. We began to apply every temporary fix that came to mind so that I could simply survive the trip home in order to find permanent healing. The male nurse was concerned and a little miffed.

MALE NURSE: *You do understand that this is crazy.*
MARK: What is?
MALE NURSE: *Staying. You get a mortal wound every seven minutes, and you still want to stay.*
MARK: I don't want the wounds. I just want to finish.

MALE NURSE:	*But you're bleeding! And, yes—I know we're supposed to bleed for these people symbolically, but don't try to turn that into some bizarre self-flagellation theory.*
MARK:	That is exactly why we're staying.
MALE NURSE:	*You don't actually think ...*
MARK:	No. I don't actually think there should be intentional physical pain. But I also don't think we should run from it. I've been here fourteen times. And at least a half-dozen of those, I did everything I could to avoid the pain. Not just the bleeding, but the headaches and the heartaches. I would do what I thought a missionary is supposed to do. But I always had a stopping point. A place of pain that would consistently cause me to retreat. Those times, I would have left by now. I can't go back there.
MALE NURSE:	*Okay.*
MARK:	So fix me up as best as you can.
MALE NURSE:	*Actually, that should just about do it.*
MARK:	Don't tell the others.
MALE NURSE:	*Why?*
MARK:	They need to figure it out for themselves.
MALE NURSE:	*When did you?*
MARK:	When did I what?
MALE NURSE:	*Figure it out?*
MARK:	The very first time I bled for Mexico.
MALE NURSE:	*I thought you said you've never had an accident here.*
MARK:	It wasn't an accident. It was a bloodletting. Completely intentional.

*flash*BANG

197

MALE NURSE:	*Why?*
MARK:	Because she needed it
	right there, right then—
	and Jesus sent me to help her.

She was losing blood quickly, and the hospital had a drastic shortage. There were two physical queues of people inside the hospital. One line of perhaps three or four individuals giving blood, whatever they could spare. The other line wrapped around several hallways. These people were waiting for the blood for their loved ones within these same walls. Survival was only available on a first-come, first-served basis.

Blood could only be given to someone who did not have a representative in line if the person who donated the blood designated the donation to that individual.

I was afraid of the comment, even as it seeped out of my lips.

You want me to donate blood to your mother?
No.

I breathed a sigh of relief, followed by a wave of guilt. The women only wanted our prayers. They would never ask us to take that sort of risk. Besides, it would be impossible for us to give blood to their mother.

Why would it be impossible?
Because her blood is too rare. She can only accept one type.

And that is when I realized that it was God directing me toward those two women in the crowd. I had thought it was my own laziness. I had not realized that God had utilized my laziness for His own plan.

I am AB Negative.

The words hung in the air for about thirty seconds as both young women dropped their jaws and stared. They began to cry once again and to thank Jesus, who had clearly sent us.

Will this save your mother?
It will help. Let us talk to the doctor. He had said it would take two AB Negative donors. We will have to make certain that your blood can be stored while we find another donor. Hopefully, it won't go to someone else.
Oh.

And that is exactly what I was feeling. Oh. How could this be? I risked so much by putting the words out there. Those scary, magic words, "I am AB Negative." It was one of the most profound, nightmarish moments of my existence. I did what I had always been hesitant to do. I had stepped out afraid and leveraged something of value to me for the good of someone I did not even know. Wasn't this the whole point of following Jesus? How could it end in futility? I was being obedient! I was risking! I was bloodletting! How could the blood not save their mother?! GOD!

THIS IS A MISTAKE!
GIVE IT MEANING!
DO SOMETHING!

Wait.

And that was the precise moment that my friend, Jonatan the missionary, spoke the five words I least expected.

"I am AB Negative, too."

five folded fingers
—OR—
WHY YOUR ZOAR IS THERE

My friend John sings show tunes. This is not his career, though I'm certain he would welcome that possibility. He sings constantly. He sings everything that crosses his mind. He sings information and questions. He sings songs he doesn't realize he has heard before. He sings when he thinks he is silent. He never stops singing. I make this clear because John is not one to be weighted down with dread.

John's heritage is the nation of Israel. He has taken many excursions to this homeland and adores every inch of the ground he has walked upon, knowing it was where Christ walked. I make this clear because John is not one to dislike any part of the Holy Land.

But, upon one specific incident, John found himself in this very state of dislike. He had traveled from Israeli town to town, absorbing the experience, meeting the locals, telling them Seinfeld is Jewish, and asking if they had ever seen *Yentl*. But the moment he passed through the border of one town, he felt a distinct sense of dread. He had an immediate aversion to the place. It was heavy, burdened, darker than any part of Israel had ever felt to him.

The town was named Zoar.

John wandered about with the feeling that something was not right. The joy had been sucked from this place—and only this place. It was as if Zoar were cursed. Upon departure, John located one of his scholar friends in order to discover why a person who adored every other inch of the nation would feel disdain for a relatively small area with no explanation. The answer was surprisingly quite simple.

Zoar was not supposed to be there.

Until I turned twelve, I shared a room with Dav. This worked very well on all the fun and brotherhood levels. Where it never did truly gel was in the compatible levels of cleanliness. I had all the makings of an anal retentive while Dav had a tendency to allow belongings to overwhelm the space they were in. Eventually, these things would overflow from a home base somewhere near the center of his trundle bed. The carpet was not visible, and oftentimes dirty laundry would be literally intertwined with electrical cords and old sandwiches, creating an environment where not one single item could be removed without creating a sort of avalanche.

The only difference in his room post-college was that somewhere in the later maze of filth a ferret was planning a family.

I can see now that I must have been the quintessential irritating brother because I was so irked by this conglomeration of items, I often shoved everything he owned over to his side of the room. This created a literal Mason-Dixon line for our civil war of rubbish.

Every area of my side of the room was spotless. And by spotless, I mean to say that I am surprised I had friends. Dusted, vacuumed. Every cassette in alphabetical order, separated by both genre and artist.

Yes. I agree. This was disturbing behavior for an early teen.

But most disturbing was the fact that my room was not

*a façade of clean, as so many others were. There was
no disaster hidden in the closet or stuffed under the
bed. Every single square foot that I had reign and rule
over was spotless. So clean that it had to be covering for
something.*

*For years, my family called me a perfectionist. A
neatnik. They labeled me as someone who needed
everything in order at all times. This was incorrect.*

*It had always perplexed my mother how I could be such
a purist in this area and yet be suspended from school
twice for cheating. The two did not line up in her mind.*

*There were many areas of my life that were sloppy. My
focus. My study habits. My mind.*

But not my room.

*I did not clean my room because I was perfect. I did not
clean my room because I was better.*

I cleaned my room because I was afraid.

Thousands of years before John set foot within its borders, Zoar had
been a stone's throw away from the big nasties. Two cities whose names
have become synonymous with bad news: Sodom and Gomorrah. The
Bible chronicles these cities as locales consumed with debauchery and
selfishness—a group of inhabitants who had chosen to so forget God that
they lived as if He could not affect them in the slightest.

There was one man with one family, however, living within these borders
who had not completely forgotten God, though the grip of the cities was

pulling stronger on him by the day. His name was Lot, and where he could have been famous for being a lone survivor, he is instead notorious for having a condiment for a wife.

You see, the angels of the Lord appeared to Lot and told him to get out of the cities NOW. To take his loved ones and escape to the mountains. At that very moment. God was going to destroy this place because of its wickedness.

But Lot hesitated. Until morning, in fact.

The angels were insistent. *Get out of here right now.* And Lot continued to hesitate.

So the angels seized the hands of Lot, his wife, and his two daughters and rushed them to safety outside the city gate. Then the angels issued an urgent warning.

> *Run for your lives!*
> *Do not stop anywhere in the valley!*
> *DO NOT look back!*
> *Escape to the mountains, or you will die!*

Lot was grateful, but in this state of emergency he took the time to protest that he could not go to the mountains because—in his opinion—disaster would catch up to him there, and he would soon die. The mountains were big and foreboding. Regardless of what God said, in Lot's opinion, it did not seem safe. Instead, Lot came up with an alternate plan of his own.

> *See, there is a small village nearby.*
> *Please let me go there instead.*
> *Don't you see how small it is?*
> *Then my life will be saved.*

But small does not always equal safe.
And near does not always equal best.

That village in question became known as Zoar.

The angel conceded. He said he would grant the request and that he would not destroy that little village after all. But Lot and his family had to hurry. To hurry and not look back.

Fire and sulfur rained down from heaven that day.

It was quite a spectacle and, ultimately, a distraction.

A distraction that caused Lot's wife to turn around for a lone glance that turned her into a statue of salt.

Now, much has been debated concerning the fairness of the wife's comeuppance. OF COURSE she would turn around and look back! It was RAINING FIRE, for crying out loud! How could God possibly expect them to be able to run away during a firestorm without looking back?!

But God did not expect them to run away during a firestorm without looking back—because God did not expect them to run away *during* a firestorm at all. Had they obeyed God's version of the plan, they would have been gone long before the fire fell.

God had demanded that they run away *the night before* anything had happened. In a window of time it would have been quite easy to escape without a backward glance.

No brimstone falling.

No light source to illuminate what had imprisoned them.

But this was not the window of opportunity that Lot and his wife embraced. They delayed and departed at the last possible moment, barely saving their skins.

Could they have made it without a reverse glimpse?

Perhaps.

But they put themselves in the worst possible situation to be tested by taking their plan instead of God's.

There was, of course, another aspect of God's orders that Lot had taken issue with. The choice of where to make the escape. God's choice had been the mountains. Lot's choice had been Zoar. Keeping with His reputation to allow us to make our own choices, God did not destroy the village that should have been obliterated. Instead, He sanctioned His angels to escort Lot and his family there.

But they would not remain there for long.

It had begun when I was much younger. Cleaning every crevice in my closet and underneath my bed for one reason.

I had to be certain there was nothing scary in there.

I had to know I was safe. I would do a sweep of the room every night before bed. I would check behind every drape. Lift up every stacked towel. Turn off my lights and stare out my window down the road in each direction. Checking to see if anything lurked in the shadows. If anything moved.

I would often remain awake as a small boy until one or two in the morning when I was certain my parents were asleep. I would then climb out of bed and do a silent safety survey of the house. Every door locked. Every window sealed. Every appliance off. Again, staring out the window for any movement. Sometimes staring for ten to fifteen minutes, convincing myself I had seen something or someone out there in the dark.

I never knew what I was looking for, but I needed to know that it was not coming.

As I grew older, it became habitual. Everything had to be in its place—in the position I knew it belonged. Everything had to be under my control.

I began to think through future horrible scenarios that might happen to me or my family. I considered every option, processed them, and prepared myself emotionally so that nothing could ever unhinge me.

Under my bed.
In my closet.
In my mind.

Everything had been stored away, locked down, and
forbidden to move.

My surroundings were familiar. Known.
Safety was always at an arm's length.
I had enough information to be free.

And yet freedom did not come.

So, why should Zoar have suffered in the first place? Why was it originally a part of the path of destruction? What had it done wrong?

Certainly just being *near* the problem area was not enough to deserve doom and destruction.

Or was it?

After all, Lot had been a godly man now tarnished. For more than a moment, he resisted rescue. Though he *loved* God, he responded as if he adored the familiarity of his city more than he *trusted* God. His nearness to what God detested grew like a cancer inside him with each passing hour.

He had convinced himself that he could remain separate while being entirely enmeshed. So enmeshed, in fact, that when the angels grasped him by the hand and pulled—his fingers would not fully let go of that which he needed to escape.

He knew he must depart, and the majority of his body did just that—but those fingers. Oh, those fingers. They could not release. They could not allow every ounce of this land to disappear.

So one end of Lot remained connected to Sodom while the angels pulled the rest of him toward the mountains. But, as those five fingers were never unfolded, the difference of his body length would only land him so far as Zoar.

This is what the enemy does. We believe that he grabs onto our wrists as we wrestle and bleed away. But, in actuality, he convinces us to hold onto him. It is our five folded fingers that hold us captive. No one else's.

God had commanded Lot to never look back at the cities.

Never.

So, why on earth would Lot choose to live where those cities could be seen every day? Where the forbidden view was right outside his window?

Lot could have followed God in the dark of night to a place in the mountains where his previous disaster was out of eyeshot—trusting God that he did not really want to be back there until he had enough distance from his desire to regain his senses.

But, instead, he chose to live within arm's length. Even as the fire fell, he refused to loosen his grip. He was plucked away, but only as far as a body length.

After a short time, Lot and his daughters had to escape Zoar because they were afraid of the people who lived there. Smaller, nearer, and easier did not result in success after all.

And where did they end up running?

To the mountains.

Only now, there was no angel to lead the way.

Lot, like every one of us, was destined to bleed. His journey would have its share of pain and growth. But there are always two ways to grow:

> 1. Resist and suffer.
> 2. Bring it on and move through it strong.

The difference between the two is five. Five folded fingers.

Either gripping as tightly as humanly possible—
Or loosening to let God's plan lead the way.

I have always been raised to keep an eye on my mountain. What is God's plan for my life? What are my aspirations? Where am I truly headed?

I have also been raised to be aware and wary of my Sodom and Gomorrah—that which would lead me to destruction.

But I had never kept an eye on my Zoar: the place in between keeping me invisibly attached to the wrong and noticeably distant from the right.

To prevent residing in that village, I would be required to choose the path of growth—of intentional bleeding. I could no longer stand the safe course where every closet was double-checked and every door double-locked. I could not be in control, and I could not choose my comfortable, safe path.

I could not follow a surprising God in a world of just-so.

I could not follow Him only to the places I was prepared to go.

Freedom would only come when I followed Him to the messy, frightening places. The unlocked and the dark. The shocking and the hidden.

And I had to follow, knowing full well that somewhere along the way, I would definitely be required to bleed.

remov ls
BEFORE
THE STATE OF EMERGENCY

The second time Kaysie dialed 9-1-1 that year was much scarier than the first. Because, the second time, she was not calling for me.

Morgan was an infant and had been running a high temperature for more than a week. She would go a few days with a low-grade temperature and then she would be fine. We had taken her to the doctor twice, but the cause of the fever was not revealing itself. This worried us more than anything because a parent has a desperate need to know what is ailing the child. This is the only way to attempt to fix the problem.

I was training a drama group across town when Dav walked into the room unannounced. He had an odd stare about him.

DAV: *Don't panic.*

As painful as these words are when one's house has been robbed, they induce a deeper level of anxiety when one knows his little girl has a fever.

DAV: *They're taking Morgan to the hospital.*
MARK: Who are they?
DAV: *The ambulance.*

A seven-month-old cries and cries, and this is horror for the parents when pain is involved because the child cannot sit up and simply tell you where it hurts. But there is something far scarier than the cries.

When the child stops crying.

Morgan's fever shot up suddenly to above 106 degrees. She was lying, lethargic and silent, in a cool tub of water. She was barely responding.

I hurried to the hospital to discover that she had a kidney infection. It had evidently been there for some time, undetected. Our physician gave her a shot and sent us home with antibiotics.

Her tiny body absorbed the prescription and struggled against the infection back-and-forth for three weeks until we arrived in Colorado to visit Kaysie's parents. The evening we arrived, her fever spiked again: 105 degrees. We hurried her a second time to the emergency room.

The doctors were at a loss. They did not know what to make of her condition. There was only one course of action that could be recommended. The doctors needed to make certain there was not a deeper problem. In order to make this assurance, they would need to draw large amounts of blood for testing.

And due to Morgan's age, this would require that they place her in a straitjacket and that I—her father—hold her screaming body down.

You didn't really.

I had no choice.

You held your own baby down while they stuck a needle in her?

She stared into my eyes and screamed bloody murder.

How could you do that?

How could I not do it?
It was either that or allow her to get sicker and sicker.
Certainly, I wished we had found another way.
That the less intrusive tests had worked at the right time.
But, at that late moment of danger, there wasn't another choice.

Was there a deeper problem?

No, just the kidney infection. But it was a very bad infection
because it had gone on for so long.
It felt like I had betrayed her. Like I was hurting her.
I wanted to scream: "I didn't do this to you! It's something inside of you,
and nothing else has been able to remove it!"
But her eyes told me that she blamed me.
The doctors swore to me that she
would never recall that moment.
That she was too young to remember.
But I can't get it out of my mind.
That's probably why we were so careful with Jackson.

Jackson?

My oldest boy. When he was four, we realized he was going to need
to have his tonsils and adenoids removed because he could not
breathe well. Fortunately, with him, we found out and planned
for the removal before it became a state of emergency.

And that was less painful?

No. Actually, with Jackson,
it was lengthier and very painful for him.
But there was never fear because he understood.
He knew a removal needed to take place.
It was as much his decision as ours.
And he knew that he needed to
prepare himself for the window of healing.
Morgan's removal was against her will in a state of confusion.
Jackson's removal was by his decision before it became crisis.
It was so funny. Because Jackson is a thinker.
For a four-year-old, he posed the most perplexing questions.

*flash*BANG

What sort of questions?

The sort that no dad can logically answer:

JACKSON: *When I grow up, can I wear a monkey suit?*
MARK: Sure.
JACKSON: *Can I have your office when you die?*
MARK: Maybe.
JACKSON: *Do sharks poop on people?*
MARK: No.

This last question was especially tough because when I answered "no,"
Jackson did not believe I had ever been in a situation
to observe this for myself.

What if a person was swimming under a shark,
and the shark had to go real bad?

Exactly Jackson's point.
But Jackson was correct in the fact that I did not
always answer his questions from the vantage point of certainty.
And his questions, when I told him about his impending surgery,
confirmed this fact to me in a new way.

JACKSON: *What will it be like?*
MARK: The surgery? Well, you won't be awake.
JACKSON: *Will it happen at night?*
MARK: No. It will take place in the morning.
JACKSON: *I got my stitches at night.*
MARK: I know, but this will be in the morning, and the
            doctor will give you something to make you fall
            asleep so that you won't even know you are in
            surgery.

JACKSON:	*Will it hurt?*
MARK:	Your throat will be sore for a while, but guess what?
JACKSON:	*What?*
MARK:	You'll get to eat all the ice cream you want.
JACKSON:	*Oh.*
MARK:	And when you get all better, you won't have a hard time breathing anymore. You won't have to make those sounds with your throat that you don't like. And the doctor says you'll be able to grow taller! And run faster!
JACKSON:	*And—and will I be able to hear God better?*

Wow.

I know.

You're kidding. He actually said that?

He said exactly that.

And what did you answer?

That would be the problem.

Please tell me you didn't say "no."

I said "no."
No, it's not that kind of an experience.
This would fix his body only.
But I was wrong. Very wrong.
I should have known better. But I said "no."

Was the surgery hard on him?

It was very hard. But he was so strong.

Because he was prepared.

I had told him what the surgery would do, and he said "okay."

And Kaysie and I were so proud.

But you should have said "yes."

It's always the hard stuff that helps us know God better—

or, at least, it's the hard stuff that affords us the opportunity.

I don't know that I always take it.

For every malady that I've reported in this book,

some I learned from at the time,

but others are only affecting me now as I write about them.

I should have given Jackson that wisdom.

I should have said "yes."

The conversation should have gone like this:

MARK: And when you get all better, you won't have a
         hard time breathing anymore. You won't have
         to make those sounds with your throat that you
         don't like. And the doctor says you'll be able
         to grow taller! And run faster!

JACKSON: *And—and will I be able to hear God better?*

MARK: If you look for Him in the pain, my son.
         My precious son.
         Life is going to throw you curve balls.
         It's your choice to either swing hard
         or blame the pitcher.
         I've blamed the pitcher, the doctor, the preacher,
         the client, the backstabbing friend—
         too many times.
         Swing for the fence, my boy!
         Bust the seams off that ball!

Don't bleed on accident.
Give it freely.
And I'll be there to shed the tears with you.

When we returned to the Mexican hospital a few days later, we discovered that the mother of the two girls did indeed live. They said it was the blood of the two AB Negative missionaries that saved her life.

On the other hand, my forearm was still sore from where they had stuck the needle that had the circumference of a McDonald's straw.

I was honored to have been the bearer of life—real life—not the flashbang I had been when I ministered selfishly before. Here in this corner of Juarez, I had left genuine teethmarks. But I had only been able to give because something living had first been extracted from me. Something painful that needed to be released. Something I had resisted abandoning until the moment it actually hurt the most.

Because of that sacrifice, she was free.

Yet there was still something holding me back from the same freedom. Something deeper that I should have released in its time by my own decision.

But I had waited.

And grown more filled with anxiety and fear. More insulated and hesitant. Those around me were being reached, but I myself was not.

It was time for that which was holding me back to be released. And the journey would not end without its share of pain.

*slap*HAPPY

I was startled wide awake by silence.

It was pitch black. My eyes focused, and I could see that the clock was creeping past five in the morning. I wanted to lie back down and drift away, but there was an inexplicable knot in my stomach. I sat motionless, and I listened.

Nothing. Complete silence.

I eased myself out of bed and stood—again listening for nothing in particular but feeling uneasy nonetheless. I could not explain why the feeling of nausea came, but I knew instantly that I needed to hurry into Morgan's room.

I eased the door open. She lay in her crib, sleeping peacefully. But something else was astir.

I heard whispers.

My heart was racing as I crept along the floor to the window of Morgan's room that faced the alley between our house and the next. I stood and eased two slats in the shades apart.

On the other side of the glass was a man. Dirty with yellow eyes filled with fury. He did not move but stood, glaring directly at me—the two of us separated only by a thin sheet of glass.

I squeezed the shutters tight and drew a breath.

There was a monster on the other side of my daughter's wall. And he was staring me down.

braving the fall

Hello. I'm back.
Oh, yes. Hi. And you are?
The boy. The boy selling the perfume samples?
Oh. Yes. You were that nice boy in the house
with the van from the Christian school—
Thank you for your purchase.
Well, that's very kind. Did you sell much?
No. I ended up using all of the little bottles on myself.
At least that's something.

So, here you go.
Here I go what?
Here are your three bottles of perfume.
The shipment came in.
But I don't need them.
What do you mean? You paid for them.
Why don't you need them?
You know why.
I'm afraid I don't.

Because I'm not real.
Excuse me?
I'm not actual. I'm a mixture of experiences
you added up for the sake of storytelling.
I only exist in this book. I have no need for perfume.
No. Wait—
Yes, Mark. It's true.

But—we met—we talked—
No. We met and talked in this book.
But, I remember—I really did use manipulation
to try to sell the perfume.
Yes. To someone. And someone else recognized you
from that Christian school. And someone else
bought enough bottles to keep you pushing on,
but they were not all the same person—and none
of them were me. I'm just an amalgamation of
everything you learned through the experience.
No. The guy said he was calling the cops,
and I ran, and then I went to your house. Right?

Why don't you think about that for a moment.
It's not a problem. It's still what you learned;
you're just gluing it all together the way we all do
into a cohesive whole.
Have I done that anywhere else in the book?
Well, you've stretched the truth into humor a bit—
altered conversations for the sake of a laugh—but the
facts are all there. They truly happened.
Yes. Right. The gall bladder, the Bell's palsy—
I remember—it all happened.
And Romania, Mexico, the shock therapy, the president
of the United States, Asian missionaries, birds dying
in spaghetti, giving blood—it's all true.
Yes. All true.
Though I believe when Henry the finch returned
to your father a year later, he landed in the neighbor's
garage rather than on your dad's shoulder.
Yeah, but that's not as exciting.
Agreed.
Whoa. I'm not a liar. That's a relief.

But, there is one pivotal moment that did not happen
at all as you have recalled.
Really?
Really.
If I'm not remembering it right,
it can't be that important.
It is of the utmost importance.
I don't know what you're getting at, because I'm
quite certain the information I've given is—

Cut the bull.
The moment that is not accurate was intentional
because you would rather not tell that story.
Rather not tell the story?! I've exposed a moment
where I defecated in front of our nation's leaders!
How could I be more unguarded than that?

You didn't mind telling that story because you still
came out looking good. What you have omitted is the
story where looking good is an impossibility.
When I ran.
You ran from the man in the neighborhood
who was calling the police.
I ran to another house. Right? I hid, and then I ran.

You ran.
But you did not run to another house.
I was afraid the man was serious.
I needed to hide. To escape.
Where did I run?

Into the woods, Mark.
You ran into the woods.

Just a little further back, I knew there would be a clearing that adults did not know about. I had been to that part of the woods dozens of times. It was always where we ran—always where we hid. It was just another hundred yards back, through these bristles and beyond the—

What's this?

I looked down into a clearing where bushes had been moved aside. A location obviously frequented by a small group of people. But what kind of people? There were empty cans and debris. And something there under that hedge. It was wet by the rain and yet blowing in the breeze.

I stepped forward to take a closer look.

A magazine.

A crumpled, weathered magazine in the middle of the woods. The wind blew two pages back and forth, exposing my eye and my mind to a hint of what was inside. I knew in my heart that it should remain untouched, but something drew me in between its pages. I imagined there would be photos that I had never seen before. What I did not imagine was that those pictures would have claws and talons that would hook into my young and fragile human heart and just tug enough to rip a slight opening. A rip that would feel warm and uncomfortable—that would bring a mixture of thrill and guilt that would slowly haunt and attempt to define me, siphoning true love and emotion out of my otherwise innocent nature as it consumed my thoughts.

In those few seconds I flipped through the pages, it was as if years of goodness drained out of my heart. My face was flushed. I dropped the magazine to the ground and ran.

I stood about fifty yards away, glancing back at the clearing. Wondering who would have bought such an awful thing and perplexed as to why they left it there on the ground. My gaze finally broke, and I walked slowly, step by step back home—each step heavier and more condemning. Growing older with each corner of my neighborhood. I had left the house that afternoon a saint and was returning a sinner, and the weight of the world pressed my soul closer and closer to the bottom of my shoe.

As days and weeks passed, I would obsess.

Why oh why did I ever run into those woods?
Why oh why did I pick up that magazine?

And suddenly, a thought I did not expect.

When oh when can I sneak back there and do it again?

But when I returned, the magazine was gone. This was a relief for the moment, but the images continued to burn in my brain. The guilt was so heavy, yet the guilt had disappeared momentarily while I gazed at the photos themselves. I needed to see more. I began to look for new ways to discover new pictures: hiding in the aisle of the drug store, going to a friend's house and jamming the cable box. It burned my innocence away bit by bit. And I slowly grew further from my family, afraid of my secret. The talons in those pages had been like the teeth of a werewolf—not just wounding me, but turning me into something I despised every full moon.

This went on for years. The cycle: craving, action, guilt, paranoia.

Until finally, one morning, I simply couldn't take it anymore. I was depressed and alone in my mind—feeling so far away from God, so depraved that He would never want to spend time in my black heart. I cried out to God. I had read about Gideon's fleece and felt it allowable for me to throw out something similar. My bedroom was always locked. Everyone knew to knock.

God—if you want me to tell someone,
let that someone walk in my door without knocking
within the next ten seconds.

That exact moment, my mother opened the door to my room.

My mother? Please, not my mother!

I trusted her completely. But I knew she considered me next to perfect. After all, I was the clean one. There's some irony for you. I was labeled "the clean one" while my mind was in the gutter.

I considered the fleece granted.

I stopped my mom from her cleaning, and I opened up my soul. I had not realized how deeply the wounds ran. I wept. I confessed everything as if I were a good Catholic. I had committed the one sin every young man is warned about. I had fallen. I began to explore verbally why these issues were burning inside of me. My father joined the conversation later in the day and began to shed light on my pain. I realized that my loneliness had come from many places. Rejection from girls. A deep-seated fear of becoming overweight.

The pictures had not been the problem.

The pictures had been the wrong answer to a much deeper problem.

I was addicted to perfection. I wanted to look, be, seem, feel perfect to everyone. I was afraid to be incorrect. I was afraid to be unforgivable. I needed to win the love of family, friends, and God.

Because I did not love myself unless I earned it.

And now I had developed an addiction so atrocious that I considered it a cancellation of all I had attempted to earn. That God was daily erasing chalk points in His big black book for everything wrong I had done or thought.

I felt hopeless and helpless.

My parents saved my life that day. That long day that ran into evening. But my own head and heart would need much more work.

I had listened to their explanation, and I had heard their love, but I was having trouble forgiving myself. Why wasn't it going away in my mind? Why were these images still haunting me? I had been honest! I had been vulnerable! God, I feel guilty enough without the pain continuing!

HELP ME!

I would run back to my mom and dad repeatedly, confessing new impure thoughts and new remembrances of sin every few days, every few hours— ANYTHING to exorcise the demons of my imagination. Honesty had been realized, but grace was hidden. Guilt raided the circus of my mind, breaking the tentpoles and ensnaring the sinful imaginations into a huddled, muddled mess.

My parents attempted to help, and their words soothed, but there was nothing more that they could do.

So I tried to live exactly by the book.

Overcome past sin by present perfection.

But it only served to alienate friends and brothers even more.

And my insecurities returned in full force, speaking to me with lies that were very convincing.

> *They didn't love you wrong.*
> *They don't love you right.*
> *You're better off doing wrong.*

I resisted. I wept in my bedroom. I told myself there had to be a balance. A balance that would grant me peace. Please PEACE! I would cry out like a banshee with longing: PEEEEEEACE!

But peace did not come because I kept on pretending.

Pretending I could be and should be perfect.

I swept my anxiety and the fear of others' knowledge of my past sins under that clean bed and into that clean closet. My college years were fast approaching. And I realized that moving away from home could bring an all-new definition to my life. I would no longer be known by a few as the sinner and by most as the suck-up. I could welcome my talents back to the forefront. YES! The comedy, the acting, the writing. I could throw my mind into those pursuits. I could disappear into other labels. Make new friends who did not know me before. No one would ever know.

And that is exactly what I did.

I disappeared into my abilities and gained notoriety in every field I touched. I became known as a success, carefree, the one you would want to become. But inside something was brewing. Because I had not dealt with the real issue. I had not dealt with the monster on the other side of the pane of glass. What was most damaging was that I was afraid to deal with it. I was afraid to even acknowledge these past (and sometimes present) imperfections. Afraid of what would be thought of me. I was thriving at a Christian college. Everyone here was blameless. Yes, I was aware of the faults and sins of others, but I knew that mine were different. Unpardonable. So I became a full-time actor—both on and off the stage. Putting on pretend confidence for all around to jump to the conclusion that I was just fine.

Years passed, and the anxiety built like a pressure cooker.

Then one fateful day I went back into the woods.

Only, the woods were no longer a bike ride through the neighborhood away from my house. They were much easier to reach. All I had to do was park my car, walk into my office, and turn on my computer.

And the woods were waiting for me.

Now married, as well as an affluent businessman, a filmmaker, author, and comedian—I occasionally found myself pulled back into the woods. I remained afraid of the monster on the other side of the pane of glass. Silent and afraid that others would find him there.

But I knew I could not remain silent.

God was tugging at my heart. He was saying,

Get rid of it.
You never did.
You just replaced it with fear.
That doesn't make it disappear.
It feeds it.
Be not afraid.
Be honest.
Tell the truth.

But I did tell the truth—and look where it got me!

That was years ago—and look where it got you. For a moment, you received
peace and redemption, but as the days wore on, you did not come to Me.
You went to yourself, your accomplishments, your plan. You've always run to that.
Well, look where that plan has taken you. You are walking in My fullness and in My

perfect will with your career and ministry, but your mind and heart are imprisoned
from celebrating the best parts of your life.
That day with your parents you took the shackles out from behind your back.
But you've never taken them off.
Because you've always been afraid they would be seen.

What do I do, God?! WHAT?! Just tell me!
I can't live like this!
I need an answer here!
A REAL answer!

The answer is not a mystery, Mark.
You can attempt to end the behavior all you want.
But the pattern will not disappear until the fear is gone.

HOW COULD THE FEAR EVER BE GONE?!
The only thing I'm afraid of is that people would—

That people would what?

That people would know.

Then, you know what you have to do.

So I made one of the single most difficult decisions of my life. From the very beginning of our courtship, my relationship with Kaysie had been based on honesty. Before we were even engaged, I had shared with her all that I had struggled with before. She was and is my best friend. Though I knew it would hurt her, I had to tell her that the woods had returned.

And a miraculous thing happened.

The truth to Kaysie did not result in rejection and repulsion.
It led to forgiveness and grace.

Certainly, there were many moments that it was devastating for her as my struggle continued. There were moments she did not want me within eyeshot. It was a part of me she could not comprehend. How could this man of God have this inside of him?

It was the same truth I was grieving over. How could the man I so desperately want to be do something like this? But as I forced myself to be honest and to truly deal, the talons began to loosen for the first time.

And Kaysie continued to love me.

That love and that trust led to accountability with other men: my pastor, Roger, and my close friend, Jason. Their support led to the revelation and understanding that a vast percentage of Christian men were dealing with the same issue, living in the same fear that this problem had no net, afraid to be seen as flawed or out of control. It was an epidemic that was crushing the plan of God in the men He had called to lead. An epidemic that grew in the seed of silence and shame.

And that knowledge began to strengthen and heal me.

That accountability led to a personal commitment to full-blown counseling, and that counseling led to the most vulnerable step of all: a twelve-step support group.

And now I am changed.

Fear is gone. The walls and hesitancies that truly made my ministry artificial have been lifted. Healing is here. And the truth is known. Am I still human? Must I continue to be vigilant in what I do or do not let into my mind? Absolutely. But I am well on the road to the real me.

I will not be afraid of the human that I am.

I will not feed the monster by keeping him secret.

I will not accept the lie that God is waiting in the wings for me to win Him over.

I move forward knowing full well that I am imperfect.

That in that imperfection, God is in control.

And that in my honesty and relationship with Him, He will continue to make my paths straight.

I was the protector. It did not matter how frightening the eyes of this man were. I would not ignore that he was there, waiting to break in through the window.

So I opened the shutters and stared him down.

And I found, upon further inspection, that he had not been staring at me.

In the darkness, he had not been able to see me at all.

He was staring at his own reflection in the window. And he was not seething out of hatred for what was inside the house. He was furious because his plans had been ruined.

Because in my haste to fear the monster, I had neglected to notice that he was not alone.

Standing on either side of him were two police officers. One reading him his rights while the other handcuffed his arms behind his back.

freethrows of a clown
—OR—
WHAT IS NOW LEFT IN MY HAND

So truth arrives.

I had always thought that truth sounded more like justice. Indignant fingers pointing down at failure. But that is not the sound I now hear. Truth now sounds like my Morgan's laughter.

My daughter, Morgan, has a beautiful laugh defined by its extreme measure of abandon. She has always worn her emotions for all to see, and when Morgan laughs, it is real, belly-grabbing, and infectious. Eventually, her laughter works its way around the table to Jackson, Charlie (who is normally the one to have provoked the laugh), Kaysie, and then me. Our laughter then kicks Morgan into overdrive. She literally becomes breathless, falling over crying—a state of being that could only be defined as slaphappy.

Slaphappy is, of course, that moment of vulnerability when the cares of the world have been wiped away. The world may be falling apart, but it has been faced and dealt with, and there is nothing left to do but wallow in honesty and laugh. It is a state of being that most resist to their very last breath. I have come to learn that it is the only state of being where I am no longer a flashbang.

Honest abandon. Where I come to the very end of me—where there is no longer even a trickle of pretense. For thirty-five years, I have attempted to make my life work on my own. I have tried to overwhelm God into saving me, when He has already done so. It is only when I look back and discover the moments of honest abandon—when I know that I cannot do it and that God will—that I have truly left a legacy. These are the moments I have been certain that God worked through me. These are the times I have been fulfilled.

It is, in layman's terms, the difference between Romania and Mexico. In Romania, I reached out the way I had seen others reach—with little regard to what was going on inside of myself.

But, in Mexico, I was shattered into little pieces.

FINAL PAUSE
for important autobiographical information

The greatest miracle of my life came from the city of Juarez.

I should have known that it would, because it was Juarez that first truly broke me. I had resisted mission work for years out of a fear of saying or doing the wrong thing. I have always given too much credit to my own mistakes and not enough credit to God's grace.

When I finally caved and accepted the gauntlet of an excursion to Mexico, it only took six days to break me. During an outdoor service in the middle of nowhere, I huddled alone and freezing behind a nearby parked vehicle and dissolved into tears—that moment in life when everything is suddenly clarified. The staggering truth was that God loved me raw though I only chose to come to Him refined. He had been tugging at my disguise for years, but I had insisted upon clinging to it more tightly. Now the curtain was drawn back, and I was exposed muscle and bone in front of my Savior.

I returned to the same city with a drama group four years later in hopes that the layers would once again be instantly peeled away. When I arrived, I discovered that the hesitancies and masks had built up again over those years. I determined that I would not resist this time and, instead, I would throw myself into the ministry.

The primary problem facing our team was that the neighborhood where we were assigned was being terrorized by a local gang. It was this gang that they hoped and prayed we would affect. Facing a Mexican gang is not in the top five of my favorite hobbies, but, even if it were, I would have resisted this particular scenario because they were notoriously violent, and we were all wearing clown suits.

Well, not clowns specifically, but we were wearing sequins, primary colors, and makeup—thinking we would be ministering only to the local orphans.

Our team rallied. We couldn't show up in those outfits for a street gang. So we determined that we would reach out to them in a manner more logical but, for me, no less challenging.

Basketball.

I am an atrocious athlete, but even that adjective does not begin to accurately describe my lack of agility in the specific arena of basketball. I am horrible. Beyond horrible. When the teams picked players when I was a child, my imaginary friend would be chosen before me. While running down court, it is often assumed by the crowd that I am having a seizure of some kind.

But I played anyway—and over the course of the week the gang members came two-by-two, jumping into our game.

At the close of the week, the entire gang had migrated over, and they were challenging us to a game. We agreed on one condition: if we won, they would have to sit and listen to what we had to say. To our surprise, they said "yes."

We began kicking ourselves. IF WE WON?! Why didn't we say, "if we play"?! Now, we have to actually win! There was a moment of stunned silence.

Then, one member of our team began to strategize: "Well, I know the way Chavez plays, so I think I could handle him." Another piped in, "Ricardo doesn't work well under the rim; he always goes for the three," and so on. Manuel does this, Aron does that, blah blah blah.

Wait a second. We know all their names? How do we know all their names?

Well—said one of the guys—we're kinda friends now.

And it suddenly dawned on us that this was true.

IDIOTS! We were morons! Here we were, falling again into the trap of strategizing for their souls, and we had already been ministering the entire time. They weren't waiting to hear our words—they had been watching us! We were so busy maximizing our plan that we had forgotten to notice we actually cared about these guys. We had fallen in love with these people and truly wanted to do anything within our power or influence to make their lives better.

We won the game.
We actually won the game.
They were happy to listen.

And through fifteen separate one-on-one huddles, every single member of that gang made a commitment to follow Christ personally—all at the same time—without knowing the others had done so.

Why was this the greatest miracle of my life?

Certainly, to discover the breadth that Jesus can rescue others through me is a huge paradigm shift. To humble myself enough to realize it's all Him and that if I will just be the real Steele, His plan will kick into action. These are life-changing moments. But these are not the reason it was the greatest miracle of my life.

That reason lies in the chain of five events that occurred afterward.

1. *I returned a year later to meet one of the new church administrators. I was pleased to discover the orphanage had more substantial help. I inquired as to the whereabouts of the gang. The administrator confirmed that they had disbanded—many becoming prominent Christian leaders in the community. The administrator knew this because, a year ago, he had been one of them.*

2. *I heard this news alongside a member of my team named Nicholas. His life was shaken by this news and by his own experience that week in Mexico.*

3. *Nick went back to Colorado to tell his mentor Chris that he must meet me.*

4. *Chris brought me to Colorado and instantly asked if he could send a team of his kids with me to Mexico.*

5. *Chris assigned one of his workers to be my co-leader because he was certain he had heard God confirm that she was to be my wife.*

Her name was Kaysie.

God knew I had not been in the state of mind to meet the girl I really needed because I was always wearing the mask—a part of me constantly pretending. So God dragged me to another country to become the real me so that the love of my life would meet that Mark first.

We fell in love quickly and surprisingly and were engaged to be married within six weeks.

And, to my complete shock, she loved all of the versions of me.

To this day, she aims every one of those versions toward Christ, toward peace and freedom, toward forgiveness, toward my true calling. Somehow, finding the one who loved me (without pretending I had the strength alone to win her over) transformed me. It explained God to me. It allowed me to finally be truthful with myself and others. To not carry the weight of the world on my heavy heart. But, instead, to occasionally let myself have moments of slaphappy.

And now I see my life with new eyes.

A view above my own circumstances—over myself—to see God's plan outside of my tunnel vision. It was not until I rose to that height that I realized my darkness had actually been selfishness—which explained the sin I had run toward. That true slaphappy comes when I release those five folded fingers that wrap around my own plan and freefall into God's version of the desires of my heart.

As I finally open my clenched hand to view my human intention, I will see that what is truly left there is nothing. That it was always nothing. That it was not an item or a skill or an ability that God wanted to mold. God wanted to use the hand itself. He wanted to use what He made rather than what I made. But the hand had been clenched so firmly that God could do nothing with it.

> *God, my arms are now wide open. Free to reach and free to embrace. Because I have seen that when I live in that place, I leave teethmarks.*
>
> *I see that serving and leading in Your Name actually works and works for the long term when I let go and love. It is the difference between me in Mexico and me in Romania. That which is true versus that*

which is planned and plotted. One follows Your lead.
The other attempts to take the lead over.

I am finished with that.

You may now begin with me.

With all the current postmodern pining over whether or not the Bible is accurate or faith in Jesus is real—with all the debate over whether or not the Christian walk is simply emotional, I can only speak from my own *before* and *after* experience.

It is amazing to witness the ferocity with which God's teaching and plan work (like they say they will) when our attempts are **true**, when we truly love and truly care and abandon what we think is best for ourselves to sacrifice for the better of the other person. When we desperately want the other to have a full life, even when that full life is not what we thought it was supposed to look like at all. When we give everything inside of us so that the other will be whole.

In my experience, this proves that God's plan is **genuine**—and that my doubts only became accurate because I was busy standing in God's way.

This is my journey from flashbang to teethmarks.

And this is how I got over myself.

(just after 6xvii)

full circle

She laughs so hard that she cries.

Who does?

Morgan. When she gets slaphappy.

That's right. She does. That's usually the point when everyone else in the room starts laughing. Even those who have been rolling their eyes.

Interesting.

Tears have always been contagious.
But slaphappy tears are the only ones that feel good.

So—I just realized something.

What's that?

You began the journey with joy. With innocence.

Then I lost it.
I lost it big-time.

Yes—but you have it back now.
It's like the wraparound.

They do those in the movies.

Yes. You lost it young and alone.
And God gave that joy and that innocence back to you.
Through your wife. Your children. Your love.
Through the few who had the ability to burn through your brilliant disguise.

I know. I hid the truth because I thought it would be damaging.
But it was the hiding of the truth that did the damage.
It feels good to lose the disguise.

Right.
So, you probably won't be needing me anymore then.

Oh—I'm certain I'll still second-guess myself.
Question every motive.
Debate the truth to death.
I'll certainly need you for that.

You'll need someone to remind you to get over yourself.

Yes.
I'll push on toward the future truth.

And I will make certain you remember what no one should ever forget.

Now that I've tasted the teethmarks,
I couldn't bear to go back to pretending.

And so, I push on to discover new territory while following all the while. I release my grip to be led. And I choose to risk and bleed for the sake of the other. I have grown to like the taste of sinking my teeth in. Of making a true difference. It is addictive. And I am learning something new in regard to the hardships of life that accompany such a journey.

The enemy and the world will always make their strongest attempt to keep you and me ineffectual. They will weaken our bite and hamper our strength and sell us the lies that we can make no difference. Because teethmarks are the most hated enemy of the flashbang.

The enemy cannot stop our attempts. So he does his best to make certain that they don't matter. He urges us to be selfish, to bicker, to keep secrets, to become overwhelmed and depressed—to blame and take sides. To rack up points. To need to be the favorite. Anything and everything to keep us from sensing someone else's pain and doing something about it in the name of Jesus.

> *Oh, God, the wretch that I was and*
> *could so easily become! I wasted so many*
> *years attempting to win Your applause. Where*
> *was my head? Where was my heart? So many*
> *others hurting so much as I stood on the*
> *sidelines and wallowed in my narrow experience.*

> *Why have we become this way—addicted to*
> *being right and despairing from a lack of*
> *answers? Why can we not set aside the*
> *perplexing question of why You are the way*
> *You are and instead trust that Your vantage*
> *point is wider and vastly larger than ours?*

> *I want to live knowing You are **good**,*
> *regardless of what I do not know for certain.*
> *Because this I do know. You are good. So good.*
> *You take the moments of sickness and tragedy*
> *and bring me through the cloud to the light.*
> *You worry less about my momentary pleasure*
> *for the sake of the man I must become for eternity.*
> *And I question because I am only looking at **now**—*
> *and I am only looking at **me**.*

*Please. Give me an ounce of Your sight. To see time
and space and people as You see them while I am in
the moment. I have been so petty. I have chosen to
see the parasite instead of the president. I have
chosen to see the paralyzed face instead of the
pregnancy. The country instead of the people.
The needle instead of the blood. The distance down
instead of the wire keeping me from falling to my death.*

*You were there. Always there. Hoping that I would
(even for a moment) take my eyes off myself and
instead look into Yours. Because when I look into Your
eyes, I see the reflection of the others hurting around me.*

*But a new day has come. The day for which You have
been preparing me. To laugh—yes, to continue to laugh.
But to lunge and grasp with my teeth. I will bite down
cold and hard because it makes it all the more difficult
to return to the lie I once was.*

I now choose, instead, to be true.

And when I am true—I believe.

I believe that I can let go,
get over myself,
give blood,
and unwrap those I left for dead.

And that is when the real wraparound occurs.

Now, the fanfare and explosions of the world that attempt to distract and sway me have lost their luster. Their teeth and talons cannot get a grip.

So I press on until all of the flash and noise the world attempts to drum up will result in no effect on me whatsoever.

Where I was once the one weeping, wailing, and waving my arms to get the world's attention with no actual result—now the roles have reversed.

I will not be distracted by the explosions I now know are frauds.
I hear the bombs and will not be swayed.
I see the flashes and will not be blinded.

And when the enemy takes his best shot—by the grace of God, I will remain unmoved.

Because the world and I have traded places.
I am now grounded in the rock.
And because Jesus is my anchor—

It is the world who is the flashbang.

(about the author)

Mark Steele

Mark Steele is the president and executive creative of Steelehouse Productions where he creates art for business and ministry through the mediums of film, stage, and animation. He has produced and directed some of the largest live youth events in the nation. He lives in Oklahoma with his wife, Kaysie, and their greatest productions: Morgan, Jackson, and Charlie. Mark welcomes your feedback at mark@flashbangbook.com.

[RELEVANTBOOKS]

for more information about other Relevant Books,

check out *www.relevantbooks.com*.
